Achieving Success
THE LORD'S WAY

I dedicate this book to my beloved wife, Fernanda, who has always sustained my efforts for success and has had patience with my failings. I also dedicate it to my biggest successes, my three sons: Joel, Jeffrey, and Jason.

Achieving Success THE LORD'S WAY

TRAFFORD R. COLE, PsyD

CFI
Springville, Utah

ISBN 13: 978-1-59955-091-6

Published by CFI, an imprint of Cedar Fort, Inc., 2373 W. 700 S., Springville, UT, 84663
Distributed by Cedar Fort, Inc., www.cedarfort.com

LIBRARY OF CONGRESS CATALOGING-IN-PUBLICATION DATA

Cole, Trafford R. (Trafford Robertson), 1951-
Achieving success the Lord's way / Trafford R. Cole.
p. cm.
ISBN 978-1-59955-091-6
1. Success—Religious aspects—Christianity. I. Title.

BV4598.3.C64 2007
248.4'893—dc22

007032076

Cover design by Nicole Williams
Cover design © 2008 by Lyle Mortimer

Printed in the United States of America

10 9 8 7 6 5 4 3 2 1

Printed on acid-free paper

CONTENTS

INTRODUCTION
SUCCESS

The book of the law shall not depart out of thy mouth; but thou shall meditate therein day and night, that thou mayest observe to do according to all that is written therein: For then thou shalt make thy way prosperous, and then thou shalt have good success.

—JOSHUA 1:8

Have you ever noticed that the men and women God has called to serve him are all extraordinary people? They are men and women who not only follow with faith and determination the will of the Lord, but also have developed talents and abilities that make them stand out in the world. Nephi started as an obedient child but went on to forge ore, build a ship, write a book in a new language, establish cities, and lead a whole population. Joseph Smith was a farm boy with little schooling who learned several languages, established three different cities in the wilderness, served as mayor of the most prosperous city on the frontier, and became a candidate for president of the United States. Among our modern apostles are a world-renowned surgeon, university presidents, and many other successful men. The list of accomplishments could go on for all of the prophets, both ancient and modern.

Do you think this is a coincidence? Did the Lord just choose men of extraordinary talent, or is it possible that any man who faithfully follows God's will can develop his abilities so that he will excel and reach his maximum potential? All of us are chosen, but are we living up to the potential that we have? What does the Lord expect of us? Are we living up to those expectations? Does the Lord have a blueprint for success?

Just what might that plan be? These are questions this book attempts to answer.

Ask yourself the following questions:

- Do I feel successful?
- Do I believe that God wants me to be successful?
- What does success mean to me?

There are hundreds of books on how to obtain success. Each author has his own definition of success and his own formula for how someone can become successful. Have you ever wondered what the Lord's definition and formula are?

Here are a few definitions of success taken from current authors:

> To realize your full potential, free yourself from randomness and uncertainty. Organize your life in such a way that the probabilities of reaching your goals is extremely high. . . . Success is the ability to live your life the way you want to live it, doing what you most enjoy, surrounded by people you admire and respect.[1]
>
> —BRIAN TRACY

> It is my feeling that real success is not the accumulation of material possessions or the attainment of a position of power or prestige. Rather, it is the peace of mind that is attained only by making the effort to do the best you are capable of doing at any task in which you are engaged.[2]
>
> —JOHN WOODEN

> Success is the progressive realization of a worthy ideal.[3]
>
> —EARL NIGHTINGALE

> Success is not a specific destination; it is a *direction you choose*. It is a process, a never-ending journey. It is your constant progress toward your highest purpose, your vision, and the life of your dreams—in *all* areas.[4]
>
> —JAMES A. RAY

> A strong successful man is not the victim of his environment. He creates favorable conditions. His own inherent force and energy compel things to turn out as he desires.[5]
>
> —ORSON SWETT MARDEN

> The man who succeeds above his fellows is the one who early in life clearly discerns his object, and toward that object habitually directs his powers.[6]
>
> —EDWARD BUDWER-LYTTON

Let me ask again. Do you believe that the Lord wants us to live up to our full potential, to have clear goals in life, and to direct our efforts toward those goals? Does he want us to live our lives so that we are surrounded by people we admire and enjoy? Does he want us to experience joy? Does he wish for us to progress constantly toward our highest purposes and attain peace of mind by doing the best that we are able in every activity we engage in?

It seems to me that the Lord has asked us to do just that. He tells us to be the very best that we can be, to live to our full potential. He has asked us to develop our talents and abilities and to use them to better this world and to serve our fellow men. What do the scriptures tell us?

> Be ye therefore perfect even as your father in heaven is perfect.
>
> —MATTHEW 5:48

To me, this is an order to excel in all we do, to seek perfection in all aspects of our lives. The Lord knows that we cannot achieve this all at once, but he has shown us the way.

In the Doctrine and Covenants, we learn that Christ "received not of the fulness at first, but received grace for grace: And he received not of the fulness at first but continued from grace to grace until he received a fulness" (93:12–13). We then learn that if we keep the commandments, we "shall receive of his fulness, and be glorified in [Christ] as [he is] in the Father, therefore . . . [we] shall receive grace for grace" (93:20).

We will receive his fulness. Can there be greater success? Nevertheless, we will not receive it right away, but step by step. One of the principles that separate us from other churches is that we believe in eternal progress—eternal growth. That progress has to begin here on this earth today.

What are some of the areas in which the Lord has asked us to excel?

Knowledge—"For behold, thus saith the Lord God: I will give unto the children of men line upon line, precept upon precept, here a little and there a little; and blessed are those who hearken unto my precepts, and lend an ear to my counsel, for they shall learn wisdom; for unto to him that receiveth, I will give more, and them that shall say, We have enough, from them shall be taken away even that which they have" (2 Nephi 28:30).

And again:

"Seek ye diligently and teach one another words of wisdom; yea, seek ye out of the best books, words of wisdom; seek ye learning even by study and also by faith" (D&C 88:118).

Health—"What, know ye not that your body is the temple of the Holy Ghost which is in you, which ye have of God" (1 Corinthians 6:19).

The Lord gave us the Word of Wisdom with the promise: "And all saints who remember to keep and do these sayings, walking in obedience to the commandments, shall receive health in their navel and marrow to their bones" (D&C 89:18).

Parenting—"And again, insomuch as parents have children in Zion that teach them not to understand the doctrine of repentance, faith in Christ the Son of the living God, and of baptism and the gift of the Holy Ghost by the laying on of hands when eight years old, the sin be upon the heads of the parents. And they shall also teach their children to pray, and to walk uprightly before the Lord" (D&C 68:25, 28).

"But I have commanded you to bring up your children in light and truth" (D&C 93:40).

Intimate Relationships—"Husbands, love your wives even as Christ also loved the church and gave himself for it. So ought men to love their wives as their own bodies. He that loveth his wife loveth himself. Nevertheless let every one of you in particular so love his wife even as himself, and the wife see that she reverence her husband" (Ephesians 5:25, 28, 33).

Talents—"For the kingdom of heaven is as a man traveling into a far country, who called his servants and delivered unto them his goods. In addition, unto one he gave five talents, to another two, and to another one, to every man according to his abilities, and straightway took his journey" (Matthew 25:14–15). As we know, to the two servants who made their talents prosper, the Lord said: "Well done, good and faithful servant; thou hast been faithful over a few things, I will make thee ruler over many things: enter thou into the joy of thy Lord" (v. 23). To the servant who buried his talent because he was afraid of losing it, the Lord said: "Thou wicked and slothful servant" (v. 26). The list could go on in all the areas in which the Lord wishes us to have success and achieve our full potential. The Lord has said: "For unto whomsoever much is given of him shall be much required: and to whom men have committed much, of him they will ask the more" (Luke 12:48). This is repeated in modern scriptures: "For of him unto whom much is given, much is required" (D&C 82:3). Who on this earth has received more than the Latter-day Saints? Does the Lord expect us to reach our full potential, to develop our talents, to become the best parents, husbands, and wives possible? Does he expect us to take care of our minds and our bodies and to develop our talents and abilities? His answer is clear. Where much is given, much is required.

Does God want us to experience joy and happiness? Has he not said that this is the purpose of our existence? In 2 Nephi 2:25, we read, "Adam fell that men might be and men are that they might have *joy*" (emphasis added).

However, when most people think of success, they think of riches. They believe that success is having a million dollars, a luxury car, a beautiful home, and so on. What does the Lord have to say about this? He has told us clearly that this life, just like eternal life, is based on laws. He states: "There is a law, irrevocably decreed in heaven before the foundations of this world upon which all blessings are predicated—And when we obtain any blessing from God, it is by obedience to that law upon which it is predicated" (D&C 130:20–21). One of the most impressive lessons of the Book of Mormon is that when the people of the Lord obey his commandments, the Lord blesses them not just spiritually but materially. The people prosper. The Lord wants us to prosper and to enjoy both the material and temporal blessings that are the result of obeying the laws on which these blessings are predicated. In 1 Timothy 5:8 we learn that "if any provide not for his own, and specially for those of his own house, he hath denied the faith, and is worse than an infidel."

The Lord has also said: "Let them shout for joy and be glad, that favour my righteous cause: yea, let them say continually, Let the Lord be magnified that hath pleasure in the prosperity of his servant" (Psalm 35:27). And still, "They shall prosper that love thee" (Psalm 122:6). The Lord wants us to obey his commandments and to prosper. He blesses his people with wealth and prosperity. Nevertheless, just as the Book of Mormon tells of the prosperity of God's chosen people, it also warns us that this was usually the cause of their downfall. They repeatedly were "lifted up in pride" because of their riches. They despised the poor. They no longer served the Lord, and soon they found themselves in internal strife, war, and bondage.

The Lord offers us the blessings but reminds us constantly to not let riches be our goal. He said: "But they that will be rich fall into temptation and a snare, and into many foolish and hurtful lusts, which drown men in destruction and perdition. For the love of money is the root of all evil" (1 Timothy 6:9–10). The Lord has warned that "where your treasure is, there will your heart be also" (Luke 12:34).

He further admonishes both rich and poor: "Wo unto you rich men, that will not give your substance to the poor, for your riches will canker your souls; Wo unto you poor men, whose hearts are not broken, whose spirits are not contrite, and whose bellies are not satisfied, and whose hands are not stayed from laying hold upon other men's goods, whose eyes are full of greediness, and who will not labor with your own hands" (D&C 56:16–17). Therefore, the Lord will bless with prosperity those who obey his commandments and who obey the laws on which the blessings of worldly success are predicated. He warns us not to make riches the object of our desires, but to use the worldly riches to bless our families and other people. In Alma, we read of a wonderful example:

> And now, because of the steadiness of the church they began to be exceedingly rich, having an abundance of all things whatsoever they stood in need—and abundance of flocks and herds, and fatlings of every kind, and also an abundance of grain, and of gold, and of silver,

> and of precious things, and abundance of silk and fine-twined linen and of all manner of good homely cloth. And thus in their prosperous position they did not send away any who were naked, or that were hungry, or that were athirst, or that were sick, or that had not been nourished, and they did not set their hearts upon riches; And thus they did prosper and become far more wealthy than those who did not belong to their church. (1:29–31)

The Lord wants us to be joyful; he wants us to have success. In fact, he expects and demands that we grow, progress, develop our talents, and use them to bless others. He expects us to be the best husbands and wives possible for our spouses, that we may become eternal mates. he expects us to be the best possible parents for his spirit children that he has entrusted to our care. He expects us to seek excellence in everything we do, from schooling, to our careers, to our church work. His promise is that he will give us his fulness, that everything that he has is ours to obtain.

Back to one of the first questions I asked: Does the Lord want us to have success? The answer is a resounding yes. **The real question is: What are you doing to obtain your personal success?** How do we do it? Does God have a formula that we can use for our success? I believe he does. Let's see. Whereas many of the books written for personal success focus on the behaviors and actions that will help us achieve success, the Lord takes a different approach.

Take a sheet of paper and divide it into three columns. In the far right column, write down at least one thing that you would like to achieve. This is your "To Have" column. You want to achieve something so that you can have something. For example, you want to lose weight so that you can achieve better health, so that you can have more energy or more self-esteem or become more attractive. You want to stop the kids from fighting so that you can have more peace, feel better, and so on. The middle column is your "To Do" column. What behaviors do you have to change, or what strategies do you need to enact, to achieve that goal? If you want a promotion at work, there may be a whole series of new habits you have to establish, or new abilities to learn to achieve that goal. This is where most self-help books end. They explain how to set goals and how to create strategies to achieve them, but the most important column for the Lord is the first. Over the first column, write: "To Be." What type of person do you have to become to achieve those goals? What internal characteristics do you have to develop to be able to reach your goal? If you want to stop your children from fighting and screaming, but you do not have the patience to speak to them kindly, what will you need to develop first—a strategy or an internal virtue? If you wish to lose weight, you can start all the diets you want and make all the "to do" lists you want, but if you do not have self-discipline, what will happen? Where do you have to begin? **God's formula begins with you**. We must work from the inside out. Let us examine his words again:

> Blessed are the poor in spirit that come unto me, for theirs is the kingdom of heaven.
>
> Blessed are the meek, for they shall inherit the earth.
>
> Blessed are they which do hunger and thirst after righteousness, for they shall be filled.
>
> Blessed are the merciful: for they shall obtain mercy.
>
> Blessed are the pure in heart: for they shall see God.
>
> Blessed are the peacekeepers: for they shall be called the children of God. (Matthew 5:3, 5–9)

Each of these beatitudes lists an internal attribute of character that we need to develop. Thus, what the Lord defines as success is not *what* we achieve but *who* we become—how we change on the inside. In fact, he ends the section with the most powerful request of all: "Be ye therefore perfect even as your father which is in heaven is perfect" (Matthew 5:48). This is success! Not only do men and women who live this life with integrity, seeking to develop their talents and abilities to their full potential, become faithful children of God, but they will stand out in the world of men and obtain success in their endeavors. We are here to learn, to exercise our faith, to develop our inner qualities of righteousness, and to develop our talents and abilities in such a way as to provide for our families and for those less fortunate than we are. We are to take care of our bodies to have the energy to raise our children, bless and provide for our spouse, and bless the world. The Lord asks that we become perfect. This is a task that goes well beyond the success that most books are suggesting. Not only does the Lord want us to succeed in a worldly sense, but he also asks much more from us. He wants us to arrive at our maximum achievement and to excel, and he wants to bless us with both heavenly and worldly success. What formula does he give us for success? Does he show us the way to achieve so much? I believe that he does. Through the scriptures, through the examples of men of God, we find how we can achieve anything that is for a righteous purpose. This is the outline that follows in the coming chapters. To best use this book, decide what you would like to improve in your life. What are the areas in which you want to succeed? Each chapter will provide some examples, but this will be effective only if you use it for your own success.

On a sheet of paper, write:

What I most want to achieve is . . .

Notes

1. Brian Tracy, *Create Your Own Future Hobeken* (New Jersey: John Wiley & Sons, 2002), 7–8.
2. Brian D. Biro, *Beyond Success* (Hamilton, MT: Pygmalion Press, 1995), 35.
3. Available from www.thinkexist.com.
4. James A. Ray, *The Science of Success* (La Jolla, CA: SunArk Press, 1999), 5.
5. Orison Swett Marden, *Peace, Power & Plenty* (Cosimo Classics, Personal Development).
6. Brian Tracy, *Million Dollar Habits* (Canada: Entrepreneur Press, 2004), 151.

STEP 1
BEGIN FROM WITHIN

All progress, all achievement, and all success begin first in the mind. One of the reasons people do not succeed in what they attempt is that they jump too quickly into the project; they act before they have properly prepared the way. Our society preaches action. We pride ourselves in being doers, but too often we act first and think later. For example, more and more people are starting their own businesses. The statistics tell us, however, that 80 percent will fail within the first year, and over half of the remaining 20 percent will fail within the next two years. Little more than 5 percent survive in the end. Why? In most cases, the new business owners have not properly prepared themselves. They did not have a good plan or the proper resources, and they did not prepare mentally to achieve their goal. Interestingly, the same statistic remains for those who try to lose weight. Most people can lose weight when they follow a diet, but only 5 to 10 percent manage to lose weight and keep it off over the long term. This is not the Lord's way. God did not just take material, slap it together, build an earth, and send us down. We were with him for eons while he prepared the way, established a plan, gained consensus from the spirits in a heavenly council, visualized and created a blueprint, delegated and trained spirits to do the work, and finally had his elect spirits create the earth over many, many years, learning and improving as they went. Therefore, before you seek to achieve something according to God's formula, you must take the necessary steps or you will fail. It first begins with you. We start from the inside out. This the foundation of success:

THE STEPS TO SUCCESS

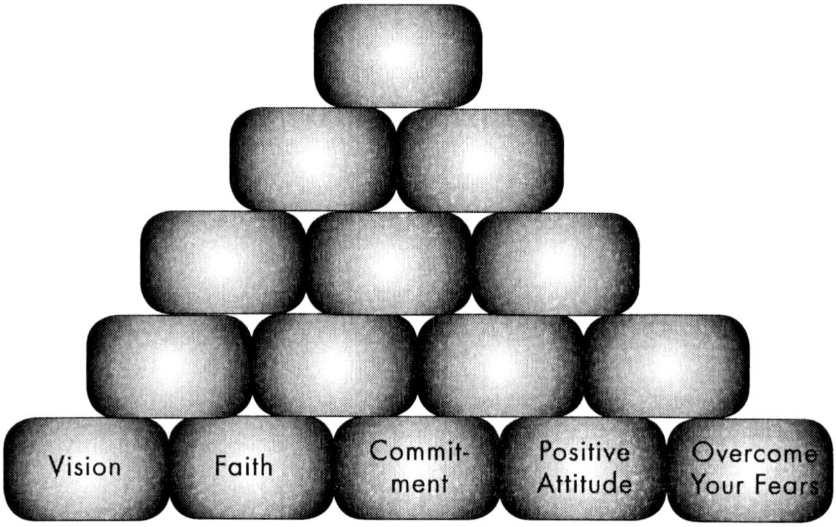

1 VISION

Where there is no vision the people perish.
—PROVERBS 29:18

In his book *The Power of Purpose,* Dick Leider describes a survey that he made of thousands of people in their old age. The purpose of the survey was to find out what, if anything, these elderly people would do differently with their life if they could live it over again. Leider asked the following questions: If you could live your life over again, what would you change? What is the wisdom you would pass on?[1] He received many different answers, but in the end, he was able to place all answers in three categories:

1. I would see the big picture. Most of the people Leider interviewed said that they were so busy living their lives from day to day that they missed the most important part of living. Their lives were so consumed with their jobs, daily routines, and petty preoccupations that they never stopped to see the big picture. They never reflected on the purpose of their life, where they wanted to go, and what they really wanted to do. The only times they did any reflection were in moments of personal crisis, and most of their life decisions were made as a reaction to these crises. If they could live their lives over, they would live according to their own personal vision.

2. I would be more courageous. Most of those interviewed stated that they ended up living their lives limited by their own fears and insecurities. Almost all stated that they would have taken more risks both in their career and in their relationships. Above all, they would have risked finding a job that was meaningful to them and that would have given them a sense of purpose in their lives. Very few had regrets regarding what they actually did with their lives, but almost all had regrets about what they never tried to do.

3. I would make a difference. Again, those interviewed lamented the fact that they could have done much more to make a difference. They desired to leave a legacy to their children and to the world. They felt that they had made little impact on the world.

Everyone should reflect on the results of this interview and ask themselves: *Do I have a vision for my life? Do I see the big picture of where I fit in and how I can make a difference with my life? What are my dreams?* Before we can achieve anything, we need to have a vision of what we want. We need to have a dream. One of the problems that many people have is that they do not allow themselves to dream. They think that it is wrong, or inappropriate, or it makes them feel bad because they do not think that they will ever achieve that dream. Yet, every major achievement in the history of mankind was achieved because someone had a dream. The Wright brothers dreamed of flying, Bell dreamed of talking over long distances; Einstein dreamed of harnessing the power of the atom; God envisioned an earth for his spirit children to come and test their faith. It all begins with your dreams and desires. What are your dreams? Write them down.

My Dreams

1.
2.
3.
4.
5.

One aspect that separates successful people from those who just remain dreamers is that successful people have a dream of what they want to achieve, whereas those who fail start with what they want to avoid but never define what they truly want. You may be unhappy at your job and wish to quit to find something else. This is not a dream until you know what you really want to do. You may hate the sight of being overweight, but your dream should not be scripted in negative terms like "I want to lose weight." Rather, ask yourself what you are trying to achieve. Are you trying to achieve health, attractiveness, energy, or youth? This will change the direction of your efforts and make your desire more positive. Have you created a life that you truly desire?

Interestingly, another survey found that only 10 percent of workers say that they consciously chose their career. Most say that they found their first job by chance through friends or acquaintances and one thing led to another so that they have ended up where they are.

The same thing can happen in every area of our lives—one thing leads to another, but we are not consciously in control. To help you find your dreams, Scott Martineau, author of *The Power of You,* suggests making a "happy board."[2] Take a pack of sticky notes and write down everything you have ever dreamed of doing and every place you have thought of going. Write anything you have ever wanted to accomplish. Write it in brief phrases in big bold letters. Do not be afraid of thinking big. Do not try to be critical or stop yourself because you think what you want is too exaggerated. Continue asking yourself, what do I want? What have I always dreamed of doing? After you write each note, stick it up on a board, your mirror, or a place that is yours. As you do this, the desires that you have repressed for years will come forth, and you should feel energized. Now divide your notes into things you want to accomplish in the next ten years, five years, three years, and what you wish to start this year. Find a few that you can begin today. Write these down in a special diary.

Once you have a dream, or many dreams, and you start to visualize it in your mind, the next question to ask is, how clear is this dream? Is it just some vague wish, or do you have a clear vision of what you want to achieve, what you want to have, or who you want to become? Many people think, "I want to work on my own." But this is a vague thought. You can start with this, but now you have to refine it. What would you like to do? How would you earn the money? Start from your vague wishes and start a true vision of where you would like to be in ten years or five years. Start adding in the details as you daydream. Do not be afraid to think big. Do not be afraid to imagine the impossible. This is where your dreams should be.

You have to think anyway so why not think big?[3]

—DONALD TRUMP

If you can dream it, you can do it.[4]

—WALT DISNEY

Most people daydream. They fantasize about how life might be if they were younger, richer, prettier, whatever. The dream, however, remains just that—a fantasy. They never take the next step to decide that they want to achieve that dream. You must ask yourself, how much do I really desire this dream? Many people spend their lives daydreaming because they never clarify the dream and they never ask themselves this question. The first step to achieving something is having a desire. You cannot achieve anything if you do not truly desire that success—not a desire of "yeah, that would be nice," but a burning desire. You must want it with all your heart, mind, and soul. How often have we said we want to lose weight but in the end we diet for a week or two and then return to our usual pattern of behavior? For twenty years, my New Year's resolution was to lose weight. Not only did I not lose any, but I gained about five pounds per year. What was I missing? Did I really desire it with all my heart, mind, and soul?

When I think of desire, I think of Ammon and his brothers, who desired to bring the Word to the Lamanites. They fasted and prayed. They studied the scriptures to gain knowledge and to receive the spirit of revelation. Listen to what was said about them: "Now *they were desirous* that salvation should be declared to every creature, *for they could not bear that any human soul should perish*; *yea, even the very thoughts that any soul should endure endless torment did cause them to quake and tremble*" (Mosiah 28:3; emphasis added). This desire allowed them to go against the advice of family and friends. It permitted them to overcome what had to be great fear at the thought of going among an enemy that had vowed to kill them. They spent seventeen years away from home, facing great hardships, being thrown in prison, and being threatened and scorned—all fueled by their burning desire.

Nephi repeats on many occasions that he desired to know the word of the Lord. He desired to see what his father had seen. This desire led him to pray, to meditate, and to ask of the Lord the knowledge that he sought: "For it came to pass *after I had desired* to know the things that my father had seen, and *believing* that the Lord was able to make them known unto me as I sat pondering in my heart, I was caught away in the Spirit of the Lord" (1 Nephi 11:1; emphasis added). Alma begins his speech on faith by discussing desire: "But behold, if ye will awake and arouse your faculties, even to experiment upon my words, and exercise a particle of faith, yea, *even if ye can no more than desire to believe*, let this *desire* work in you, even until ye believe in a manner that ye can give place for a portion of my words" (Alma 32:27).

The Lord will answer our prayers according to the righteous desires of our heart. Let the desire work in you to achieve your dreams. If you want success in your life, you must begin with true desire. If you want to lose weight to improve your health, to have more energy to work, to better serve your family, and to improve your life, then it has to become a priority. You must truly desire it. You have to desire health more than the emotional appeal of food. You will have to think about it, work on it, and dedicate great energy to this effort to succeed. You will have to change habits, lifestyle, and values. It will take great effort, and this has to be driven by your desire. You must be like Ammon and his brothers. Your burning desire must carry you through the difficult moments. Many of us have a desire to become faithful members of the Church, to perform our duties, and to seek righteousness. At what level, however, is our desire? Do we really desire to perform our home teaching? If we do, would we find a way to perform it every month? Do we have that same desire of Nephi to seek revelation and know the word of the Lord? If we do, would we find ten or twenty minutes a day to read the scriptures? When Enos had a problem and sought the answer from the Lord, did he time his prayer? No! He did not go to work that day; he was not distracted by other thoughts or commitments. His desire was so great that he prayed all the day and all the night to the Lord. When was the last time you had such a desire to receive an answer from the Lord?

The same is true for our relationship with our spouse. Most people say that their relationship is important to them; many even say that it is the most important thing in their life. But then the relationship often slowly dies from neglect and routine. If you want success as a spouse, you must make your relationship a priority. You must strive every day to improve yourself and show your love to your mate. You must truly desire a celestial marriage where love and harmony reign to overcome the fatigue, routine, selfishness, and one thousand other obstacles that the world throws in your path to destroy the family. You must have a vision of what you want your relationship to be and you must truly desire to achieve that vision. **Your desires determine your priorities**. We dedicate our energies to what we desire most. The reverse is also true. You dedicate your energies to what you desire the most, whether you admit it to yourself or not.

> All our dreams can come true, if we have the courage to pursue them.[5]
>
> —WALT DISNEY

The Lord has said, "Verily, verily, I say unto you, *even as you desire of me* so it shall be done unto you; and, *if you desire,* you shall be the means of doing much good in this generation" (D&C 11:8; emphasis added).

ACTION EXERCISES

1. Begin a journal dedicated to success, and use it while you read this book.
2. Divide your life into different areas like work, education, self-improvement, social relationships, family, spirituality, and health. Write down your dreams for each of these areas. Let your imagination run wild, dream your biggest dreams, indulge yourself in your thinking, and write down all your dreams. Come up with at least three dreams for each category.
3. Create your own "happy board."
4. Select the dreams that create the most enthusiasm in you. These are the ideas that make your heart race when you think of them.
5. Each day fill in details about your vision of how you want these dreams to come true.
6. Select three dreams that you can begin or complete within the next year or two. You should focus on these dreams as you read this book.

Nobody succeeds beyond his or her wildest expectations unless he or she begins with some wild expectations.[6]

—RALPH CHARELL

Notes

1. Richard J. Leider, *The Power of Purpose* (San Francisco, CA: Berrett-Koehler Publishers, 1997).
2. Scott Martineau, *The Power of You* (Hobeken, NJ: John Wiley & Sons, 2006).
3. Available from brainyquote.com.
4. Jeff Keller, *Attitude Is Everything* (Tampa, FL: INTI Publishing, 1999), 34.
5. Available from brainyquote.com.
6. Keller, *Attitude Is Everything*, 25.

2 FAITH

Without faith you can do nothing; therefore ask in faith. Do not ask for that which you ought not.

—D&C 8:10

You now have several dreams that you wish to pursue. You have the desire to achieve some change in your life. Many people remain just at this point. They spend their entire lives with their dreams but never act on them because they lack the faith to take the next step.

Faith is the predecessor of all action, not just religious action, but all action. The farmer does not sow if he does not have faith that the seeds will grow and produce fruit. The baker does not make bread and put it in the oven if he does not believe that it will rise and be good to eat. The salesman does not make a call unless he has faith that at least someone will buy. The teacher has to believe that some of her students will listen to her and learn new principles. Parents have to believe that the sacrifices they make will benefit their child. We act because we have faith that our action will have a positive result.

In the same way, we do not act because we lack faith that our action is worth the effort. Nephi prayed for knowledge, and his faith was rewarded. His brothers did not believe that God cared enough about their welfare to answer their prayers; they did not pray.

The scriptures are full of other examples of faith. Abraham had the faith to leave his father in Ur and venture with his family to a land that God had prepared for him. He had the faith to obey the Lord when told to sacrifice his only son, believing that somehow it was part of God's plan. Lehi had the faith to prophesy to his neighbors and others that their mighty city was doomed to fall. He did this even when they mocked him, abused him, and threatened to kill him. He had the faith to leave his comfortable home in Jerusalem, his wealth, his position, and take his family into the wilderness. He sent his sons back into danger to obtain the brass plates; he continued his journey with faith even though he saw his wife suffer hunger and thirst and rebel against him. He continued with faith even though his older sons despised him. It was this faith in God that directed every action in his life. Noah had the faith to build the ark long before the floodwaters arrived. The people made fun of him and laughed at him, but he persevered. Nephi built the boat that would take his family to America. He had never built a ship before, but he had faith that the Lord would direct his efforts and that the boat would be seaworthy.

Many of us believe that we too would have faith if the Lord appeared to us in a vision or spoke to us directly. Instead, the scriptures teach that these manifestations come after the trial of our faith. We need to first plant the seed, see the plant grow, and witness that the plant is good. We need to exercise our faith in the small matters so that we can learn how God operates in our lives. Then we will be ready for the greater challenges. Nowhere is faith described so well as in Alma 32: "And now as I said concerning faith—faith is not to have a perfect knowledge of things; therefore if you have faith ye hope for things that are not seen, which are true" (v. 21). We have hope. We have confidence that things will turn out for the best, so we act. And as we see the fruit of what we have done, we gain faith that it is true. We hold family home evening with faith that it will improve our family relations even if it seems like an eternal battle. We stay at home with the children when they are young and put off our career, because we have faith that somehow this will make a positive difference in their lives. We do not have a perfect knowledge of the results, but we hope for results that we do not see at first but that are true principles.

Many of us have faith in the Lord—we just do not have faith in ourselves. Our past experience has been negative, and we have little faith that we can change. As Mark Twain said, "I know I can quit smoking, I have done it a hundred times."[1] When I have tried a hundred diets but I never permanently lose weight, it is difficult to believe that this time will be different. When I have struggled with a problem and have fallen into the same pattern of sin again, I do not have much faith that things will change. We lose faith in ourselves each time we fail at a task. The first concept to understand is that we probably failed because we were not doing things the right way. The plan we created was not working, and we needed a new plan. This book is about taking the right steps to create a good plan that will help us achieve these goals.

The second concept is that all things are possible in the Lord. We believe that the Lord can move mountains or build a ship, but we do not believe that he can help us. I can imagine Nephi on the shores of the Indian Ocean receiving the command to build a ship and saying, "Are you kidding? I don't know how to build a ship!" That would probably be my reply. But Nephi had faith and as he had already said, "I will go and do the things which the Lord hath commanded, for I know that the Lord giveth no commandment unto the children of men, save he shall prepare a way for them that they may accomplish the thing which he commandeth them" (1 Nephi 3:7). Nephi found the faith in himself because his faith in God was so great. We have to find the same faith.

How do we apply this in our daily lives? How does faith help us lose twenty, fifty, or one hundred pounds? How does faith help us perform our home teaching or say our daily prayers? What does faith have to do with earning more money or being a better parent?

Faith works on certain principles. First, we must believe in true principles. We must learn of the true nature of God to have faith in him. Just as important, we must believe that what we are asking of God is a righteous desire. We cannot have faith that the Lord will bless us if we are seeking something for our selfish desires. Asking the Lord to help us lose weight so that we can be more beautiful and impress our friends is not necessarily a righteous desire. Asking for help improving our health to have more energy to serve our family and loved ones certainly is. In the same way, desiring to win the lottery to have a million dollars so we do not have to worry and struggle anymore in our life goes against the Lord's will because it is in the struggle that we become strong. Therefore, material success for vanity, pride, or personal gratification will not generate faith that the Lord will bless our endeavors. On the other hand, asking the Lord to bless our work that we may prosper to better provide for our family, to better use our talents, and to improve the world is a righteous desire and we can have faith that the Lord will bless us, if it is part of his plan for us.

Having faith in the Lord, then, requires that we believe that our endeavor is for a worthy cause and is according to his will. Another factor that is equally important is that before we can go to the Lord with our request, we must know that we are striving to observe his commandments. We have to believe that we are worthy of his love and attention. This is where many of us fail—either because we are not obeying his Word, or more often because we have such low self-esteem that we do not believe that the Lord cares about us. In this case, we should meditate on the scriptures where the Lord tells of his love for each of us. Meditate on this scripture: "Ask, and it shall be given you; seek, and ye shall find; knock, and it shall be opened unto you. For every one that asketh receiveth; and he that seeketh findeth; and to him that knocketh it shall be opened. Or what man is there of you, whom if his son ask bread, will he giveth him a stone? Or if he ask a fish, will he give him a serpent? If ye then, being evil, know how to give good gifts unto your children how much more shall your Father which is in heaven give good things to them that ask him?" (Matthew 7:7–11).

The Lord loves each of us; we are his children in every sense of the word. He wants what is best for us. One way to increase our faith is to sacrifice to obey his word. Each time we make an effort to obey him, we are blessed, and each sacrifice we make increases our confidence that the Lord will in turn bless us. Going the extra mile to help someone, doing our home teaching when we have no desire to do so, and having extreme patience with our children when we want to throttle them reinforces in us the idea that we deserve the Lord's favor when we call on him for help. The Prophet Joseph Smith once said, "A religion that does not require the sacrifice of all things never has power sufficient to produce the faith necessary unto life and salvation. . . . Those who do not make the sacrifice cannot enjoy this faith, because men are dependent upon this sacrifice in order to obtain this faith."[2] To increase our faith we would do well to read again those words of the prophet.

We also need to have faith in our plan. This comes with proper preparation. I can have faith that the Lord will help me teach my gospel doctrine lesson only if I know that I have properly prepared, that I have done all I could to be a good teacher. Then I can ask his help to touch the hearts of my students. If I know deep inside that I have not done my part, I have no confidence that the Lord will bless me. The more prepared I am, the greater my faith. (We will address this issue again in a future chapter.) This is just as true in business and at home. How often do we ask the help of the Lord to be a better parent without ever having read a book about parenting, taken a course, or made a plan on how to change our behavior toward our children? How much faith can we have that the Lord will intervene and change the situation? We must prepare ourselves, create a plan, and go to the Lord. Then we will have the necessary confidence that we can achieve our desires.

Intrinsic to faith is prayer. We must pour out the desires of our hearts to our Heavenly Father and ask his help. If prayer is not enough, we need to add fasting to our prayers. We can ask the Lord's help only if we know that we have done everything necessary to do our part too.

The result of true faith is optimism. You are now confident in the Lord and in yourself that you can obtain the results you desire. There is no place for pessimism in a person of faith. If you find yourself becoming pessimistic, you need to go back to the Lord with your righteous desires.

> Optimism is expecting that most things will work out to a successful completion, and even more important, that you have the power to contribute to that outcome.[3]
>
> ROGER CRAWFORD

Often, it is our own attitude that creates the outcome. This is called a self-fulfilling prophecy. When we expect positive results, we have a positive attitude. This enthusiasm will generate the results we desire. The same thing happens when we have negative expectations—those same expectations change us, change others around us, and create negative results. Napoleon Hill, one of the first and most famous authors to write about success, interviewed the five hundred richest men in America and found that the characteristic that most distinguished them was what he called "positive expectancy."[4] They made a habit of looking at every obstacle or setback as a potential for a greater advantage or benefit, and they always found it.

If you truly believe that you have the Lord on your side, could you ever be pessimistic? Fight your pessimistic attitude. Most pessimists face difficulties by ruminating over past mistakes with the passive and negative attitude of "if only"—if only I had done things differently, if only I had more funds, if only there was not a recession. This stops all action and makes excuses for our failures. Start thinking, "Next time I will." This directs your mind to future action and allows you to learn from your mistakes. Refuse to consider the possibility of failure. Work to deserve the help of the Lord. Go forth with confidence and you will succeed.

> If one advances confidently in the direction of his dream and endeavors to live the life which he has imagined, he will meet with success unexpected in common hours.[5]
>
> —HENRY DAVID THOREAU

At this point, we have the desire to become better parents, to lose fifty pounds, to start a new business, or whatever we need to do to be more successful. We believe that what we are asking of the Lord is worthwhile and righteous, and we are willing to plant the seed. We have faith enough to ask the Lord's help and begin again. The next step in obtaining achievement is commitment.

ACTION EXERCISES

1. Read your journal and examine your dreams. Meditate on each of those you have written. Select those dreams that you are ready to act on.
2. Write down your motives. Are they righteous desires? Do you believe that the Lord will help you accomplish these dreams? If you have any doubts, write them down and analyze why you are not sure. Is it the dream that is not worthy? Is it your relationship with God that is not healthy? Is it your confidence in yourself that is lacking?
3. Go to the Lord with your doubts, perplexities, and hopes. Seek his confirmation that he loves you and desires your success.
4. Make a decision to pursue your dreams, and ask his help with faith.
5. Renew your optimism daily with your prayers to the Lord. Change all your "if only" thinking into "next time" thinking.

Notes

1. Available from www.brainyquote.com
2. Joseph Smith, *Lessons on Faith.*
3. Roger Crawford, *How High Can You Bounce* (New York: Bantam Books, 1998), 33.
4. Napoleon Hill, *The Master Key to Riches* (New York: Fawcett Books, 1991).
5. Cherie Carter-Scott, *If Success Is a Game, These Are the Rules* (New York: Broadway Books, 2000), XIV.

3 COMMITMENT

Commit thy way unto the Lord; trust also in him; and he shall bring it to pass.

—PSALM 37:5

Many fail in their plan or achievement because they are not truly committed to success. What does commitment mean? It means that we will succeed no matter what. We will do everything necessary to achieve our goal. This commitment can be complete if we have first decided with the Lord that it is a worthy goal and have faith that we can achieve it. Now, deep inside of us we go beyond just desire and commit ourselves that we will do it. It is no longer "I will try to be a good husband." It is "I will do everything necessary to make sure that my spouse knows that I love her, cherish her, and honor her, and I will make whatever sacrifice needed to make ours an eternal marriage. I am committed."

It means that I will succeed in losing weight whether it takes me a month, a year, or five years. I will reach my goal. I will learn everything necessary about correct dieting, I will change my lifestyle, I will exercise regularly, and I will lose weight. Other things in life will have to take second place because this is my priority right now.

I will succeed as a salesman. I will take every course necessary, dedicate the time necessary, change my attitude, learn from other qualified salesmen, and I will succeed in selling three times what I am doing now.

Can you see what commitment does? There is no hesitation. There is no wavering. There is no compromise. I will do it. We can have this commitment only if we have taken the first two steps. I have to truly desire to achieve this goal, and I have to believe that this is a righteous desire that warrants my full attention and that the Lord is with me. I have to be totally motivated. Christ did not say, "Love God." He said: "Thou shalt love the Lord thy God with all thy heart, and with all thy soul and with all thy mind" (Matthew 22:37). This is commitment!

Elder F. David Stanley commented on the price of success: "A common ingredient among all successful people is an understanding of what constitutes paying the price of success. Basic in that formula of paying the price is an inner gift of determination that says: 'I'll do whatever it takes.' That means, 'I'll work hard, with integrity, to achieve my goal.' "[1]

In his book *Ultimate Guide to Mental Toughness,* Daniel Teitlebaum gives a very good example of this:

> I pull a hundred-dollar bill out of my wallet and pose the following challenge to you: "I'd like you to break through the wall nearest to you right now. You can use your hands, your feet, or the chair you're sitting on, and the second you carve a hole in the wall you get this one-hundred-dollar bill." Would you ruin your wall for so little? Most would say no way. . . .
>
> Take a second to think about the person most important to you in your life; one of your kids, your spouse, one of your parents. Now I'd like you to imagine that as you are sitting in your room right now, you look up to the heating vent in your ceiling to see smoke pouring out of it. As the smoke starts to fill your room, the fire alarm in your building goes off, and outside in the distance, you hear the wail of fire engines as they approach your building.
>
> Before you get up to leave, you see that the wall nearest to you starts to blacken . . . and you realize that the fire in your building is literally next door, that it's critical that you get out of your building now.
>
> Now, before you get up to leave the room, suddenly you hear the voice of that person most important to you in the world from the other side of that wall. They're screaming for help . . . and you realize that they're trapped; they can't get out; you need to save them right now. As you watch the wall continues to blacken.
>
> From knowing the layout of your building, you realize it's impossible to get to the room they're in, it's down several corridors, and too far to get to quickly. So you turn . . . and face the wall the screams are coming from. At this moment, you have no options; you've got to save that person right now.
>
> Here's my question again. Do you have any doubt in your mind that you couldn't carve a hole in that wall, using either your bare fists, the chair you are sitting in or the desk next to you?

Will you do it? Will you find a way? Will you give up? There is a shift now in motivation. Your desire is no longer lukewarm—it is

> a burning desire. You will succeed no matter what it takes. You are totally committed.[2]

In the book of Revelation the Lord says, "I know thy works, that thou art neither cold nor hot; I would thou wert cold or hot. So then because thou art lukewarm, and neither cold nor hot, I will spue thee out of my mouth" (3:15). If we are lukewarm in our desires, we are not committed and we will not achieve the success we need. In any endeavor, there will be obstacles. Things will not turn out as we want them to. Often the difference between the 95 percent of businesses that fail and the 5 percent that succeed is the commitment of the entrepreneur. If you are committed, success is a must, and you are willing to do what it takes to achieve it.

Just one example of commitment might render the idea. A few years ago, *American Way* magazine interviewed best-selling author David Baldacci. Baldacci has written novels like *Absolute Power*, *Total Control*, and *The Winner* that have sold millions of copies worldwide. David Baldacci did not start as a novelist. He graduated instead as a lawyer and he enjoyed writing. He realized, however, that he did not have very good writing skills. Therefore, he made the commitment, as he stated, to obtain those skills. For five years, he wrote character descriptions, plots, and scenes. He had a family and was working full time. The only time he had to dedicate to writing was from 10 PM to 2 AM, so that is the time he used. He wrote every day for five years. Then for the next five years, still from 10 PM to 2 AM, he wrote short stories and screenplays. He tried to sell them with no results, but he was committed so he continued. Finally, in 1996, ten years after he had started, he finally published the novel *Absolute Power*, which was made into a movie the same year, and he finally made his millions.[3] Commitment to excellence paid off. How many would-be authors have not had the commitment to learn the skills, to learn how to market their books, to face rejection, and to endure until they achieved success? It is the same in any field.

Nephi could have decided that the shores of Bountiful were a good place to live. He and his family had left Jerusalem and were safe. After many years of wandering in the wilderness, they had a land of bounty. Why go any farther?

Would we have had the Book of Mormon if Nephi had not been committed? Would we have had a second witness to Christ or a chosen people in the New World? Nephi was committed, and we have been blessed.

What if Christ had not been committed? What if he had not said,

"Thy will be done"? What if he had decided that atonement for all the sins of the world was just too much? He had already lived a perfect life. Why should he have to endure the torture of bleeding from every pore for us?

What if Joseph Smith had not been committed to restoring the gospel, even to giving his life as a witness to God's cause? All great endeavors come from the commitment of someone who wanted to achieve and did everything necessary to achieve.

Commitment, whether in the spiritual realm or material, is what makes the difference. Only when we are fully committed are we able to achieve our goals. The Lord rewards our commitment and the universe responds to our determination.

Commitment was well described centuries ago by the writer and philosopher Johann Wolfgang Von Goethe:

> Until one is committed there is hesitancy, the chance to draw back, always ineffectiveness. Concerning all acts of initiative there is one elementary truth, the ignorance of which kills countless ideas and splendid plans; that the moment one definitely commits oneself, then Providence moves too. All sorts of things occur to help one that would otherwise never have occurred. A whole stream of events issues from the decision, raising in one's favor all manner of unforeseen incidents and meetings and material assistance, which no man could have dreamt would have come his way. Whatever you can do or dream you can, begin it! Boldness has genius, power and magic in it.[4]

This is your life.

When I think of commitment in the scriptures, many examples come to mind, but Jacob stands out. Jacob sees Rachel, falls in love with her, and goes to her father, Laban, to ask her hand in marriage. Her father requests that Jacob first work for him for seven years. Jacob does, but Rachel's father first has him marry his older daughter, Leah, and then work seven more years for Rachel. Do you think Rachel had any doubt about Jacob's love for her after fourteen years of service to her father to have her? I love the scripture in Genesis that says: "And Jacob served seven years for Rachel; and they seemed unto him but a few days, for the love he had to her" (29:20). Would Rachel have any doubt of his commitment to her and their love? I think not. Can you see the difference this would make versus this proposition: "Let's live together for a while and see how things work out"? Commitment overcomes all obstacles because we are working with our full intent. We are determined and nothing will stop us.

In the words of Mary Crowley, "One person with commitment is worth more than one hundred people who have only an interest."[5]

Go back and look at your dreams. How much do you really desire to achieve them? Is there one or more dream that you can commit to totally? How committed are you to becoming a better spouse, a better parent, or a better person? What you achieve will be directly proportional to your commitment to achieving what you desire.

ACTION EXERCISES

1. Examine the dreams that you have decided to pursue. Which are you most committed to? Which will you pursue with all your heart, soul, and mind?
2. It is on this dream that you must focus your attention, your efforts, and your energy until you have achieved it. Write down in your journal: "I will achieve ________ and will work on it constantly until I have accomplished my dream." Write it in block letters that stand out.
3. Meditate on what you have just written and take it to the Lord. Confirm your commitment with him.
4. Now communicate it to your family members and the people closest to you. The more you make your commitment public, the stronger it becomes.

Notes

1. F. David Stanley, "The Principle of Work," *Ensign*, May 1993, 44.
2. Daniel Teitelbaum, *Ultimate Guide to Mental Toughness* (Silver Springs, MD: Demblin Communications Inc., 2003).
3. Jeff Keller, *Attitude Is Everything* (Tampa, FL: INTI Publishing, 1999), 41.
4. Available from www.saidwhat.co.uk.
5. Available from www.belovedheart.wordpress.com.

4 ATTITUDE

If you can believe, all things are possible.
—MARK 9:23

Whether you think you can—or think you cannot—
you are right.[1]
—HENRY FORD

Earl Nightingale, one of the greatest success writers, affirmed that the key to success in any field could be summed up in just six words: *We become what we think about!* The same is true whether we are seeking spiritual success, financial success, health, or anything else; we become what we focus our attention on. Our thinking patterns determine the type of person we are. If we want to change something in our lives, we need to begin with our thinking. We cannot continue thinking the same way and expect to change. If I have been struggling with a problem, I will not find a solution until I find new information, a new perspective that changes my thinking. If I continue with the same thoughts and beliefs that I have always had, I will obtain the same results that I have always had.

A man is what he thinks about all day long.[2]
—RALPH WALDO EMERSON

Unfortunately, it is rare in the scriptures to find how the prophets were thinking. But when we do find passages of inner reflection, it is quite enlightening. Maybe the best example of a change in thinking comes with the conversion of Alma the Younger in Alma 36: "But I was racked with eternal torment, for my soul was harrowed up to the greatest degree and racked with all my sins. Yea, I did remember my sins and iniquities, for which I was tormented with the pains of hell" (v. 12). As Alma meditates on his sins, he is racked with pain, but when he thinks on the mercy of Christ, his thinking, emotions, and actions change: "And oh what joy and what marvelous light did I behold; yea, my soul was filled with joy as exceeding as was my pain! Yea, I say unto you my son, that there could be nothing so exquisite and so bitter as were my pains. Yea and again, I say unto you, my son, on the other hand, there can be nothing so exquisite and sweet as was my joy. Yea, and from that time even until now, I have labored without ceasing, that I might bring souls unto repentance; that I might bring them to taste of the exceeding joy of which I did taste" (v. 20–24).

Previously, Alma had been actively working against the Church with his friends, the sons of Mosiah, setting a bad example and rebelling against their fathers. Look at how Alma's whole thought pattern changed. The experience of many who are converted to the Church or who have repented sincerely of their sins is similar to Alma's experience—they no longer have any desire to do wickedness but only desire to do good the rest of their lives.

Good thoughts and actions can never produce bad results; bad thoughts and actions can never produce good results.[3]

—JAMES ALLEN

How does positive thinking work, and how can we use it to obtain our own success? Many authors call this the law of dominant thought. Our dominant thought during the day remains in our attention, and we start organizing our thinking and our actions around that thought. From a neurological point of view, in our brain we have the Reticular Activating System (RAS), which is our attention and arousal center. When we leave it in neutral, it focuses attention on anything necessary for survival—hunger, thirst, danger signals, and so on. When we consciously direct it toward something, it will focus on that as though it were necessary for our survival. A simple example will suffice. Let's say you are deciding to buy a new car, and you really like a certain model. What do you start seeing everywhere on the road? All of a sudden, those cars jump out and you see them everywhere. When they do, you think about them more, admire them, and start noticing the different colors and accessories. This is your dominant thought, and your brain will keep it in the forefront of your attention center as long as it remains important for you.

> The things you think about determine the quality of your life. Your soul takes on the color of your thoughts.[4]
>
> —MARCUS AURELIUS

If I decide to achieve a goal, I have the desire and faith, and it aligns with my strengths. I now need to make this my dominant thought, and I must do it in a positive way. If I want to improve my relationship with my children and this becomes my dominant thought, I start thinking about them constantly. I will analyze my behavior and their behavior to see what I can change. I will be motivated to find information that changes my understanding about why my children behave the way they do or how I am negatively influencing them. I will start noticing how other children act. I will be interested in how other parents deal with these problems. I will pray for guidance, and this will dominate my prayers. All this will change my thinking and therefore help me change my actions. When I put into practice a new strategy with my child, this will become my dominant thought during that day or week or month until I have achieved my purpose.

In the same way, if I want to lose weight and start an exercise program, this will have to become my dominant thought during the day for many days until it becomes a habit. I will have to reinforce my decision with positive thoughts about why this pain is necessary and the good it will do me. I have to reinforce my commitment with positive thoughts. If I stop focusing on my goal and let other thoughts and interests distract me, it will no longer dominate my thinking and I will not succeed.

Similarly, if I want financial success, this too must become part of my dominant thoughts. Thought always precedes action. When you direct your dominant thought toward your goal, you begin finding the opportunities and creating the actions that move you in that direction.

> They can because they think they can.[5]
>
> —VIRGIL

Now, the problem that most of us have is that we have thoughts, but often they are negative thoughts. Inside, we are often saying to ourselves: "I'll *never* be able to lose all those pounds. I have tried a hundred times without success." Alternatively, we say: "I guess I was born to work, because money *never* comes my way." That is, our thinking is often negative. We envy others, we blame God, we complain, we justify, and in general, we do not believe that we can achieve what we want. Very often, we are not even aware of what we are saying to ourselves. We are constantly putting ourselves down, and we are not even aware of it. Not only that, but thought and emotion go hand in hand so that when I start a negative dialogue with myself even unconsciously, I change my mood and become anxious or depressed, which in turn increases the negativity of what I am saying. Most of us talk ourselves out of changing habits or improving before we even begin. What can we do to stop this and change our attitude to something positive and motivating?

There are four steps to changing your attitude toward anything:

1. Awareness
2. Understanding
3. Disassociation
4. Reconditioning

How do we start a series of positive thoughts? The first step is awareness. We should observe the thoughts we have and tune in to what psychologist call our internal dialogue. What do you say to yourself? Constantly saying to yourself words like "Look how fat I am; I am disgusting!" will not help you. Your dominant thought is about being fat, your thinking is negative, and you will remain fat. Your brain focuses on being fat and on being disgusting. This lowers your mood, and you console yourself with more food. Inside your head your dialogue continues: "I'm never going to lose weight, so I might as well relax and eat this ice cream."

Likewise, the person who is struggling in his or her career often has an equally negative dialogue. He might say things like, "I hate this job" or "I'll never get anywhere." He may also have negative beliefs about wealth. Even though most people say they want to be rich, they often have negative attitudes about the rich: rich people are greedy; rich people steal from the poor; rich people will never make it to heaven. These attitudes influence our thinking pattern, and we will, in fact, never be rich or even well off. Until you become aware of your beliefs by listening to your automatic thoughts, you cannot change them, and they will continue influencing you negatively. We must become aware of what we are saying to ourselves. Only when we are aware of what we are saying to ourselves can we change the script. The parent who deep inside believes that his or her children are a nuisance or bad will continually reaffirm this belief through a negative internal dialogue.

A good example from the scriptures of this change in one's internal dialogue comes from Nephi. Nephi is very personal in his writing, and some of my favorite passages are his internal reflections. We can read in the psalm of Nephi the following: "O wretched man that I am! Yea, my heart sorroweth because of my flesh; my soul grieveth because of mine iniquities. I am encompassed about, because of the temptations and the sins which do so easily beset me. And when I desire to rejoice, my heart groaneth because of my sins" (2 Nephi 4:17–19). This is what many of us do! We focus on our weaknesses, we beat ourselves up, and we become depressed. The difference between our behavior and that of Nephi is that he consciously and deliberately shifts the direction of his thinking. He focuses on the goodness of the Lord. Look at how his thinking has changed and become positive just a few verses later. "Awake my soul! No longer droop in sin. Rejoice, O my heart, and give place no more for the enemy of my soul" (2 Nephi 4:28). What does this tell us about his thinking and who he was? Look at the change that he consciously and deliberately makes in his thinking patterns.

There is nothing either good or bad, but thinking makes it so.[6]

—WILLIAM SHAKESPEARE

Try this. Take a small notebook with you everywhere you go for one week, and write down everything you say about yourself in your internal dialogue. Note particularly what your thoughts are when you think about the problem that you are trying to face or the area of success that you are trying to achieve. As you practice awareness, you will be amazed what you are constantly saying to yourself. It's estimated that the average person has about

60,000 thoughts a day, and most of these are unconscious and automatic.[7] Unfortunately, for many of us, most of these 60,000 thoughts are negative. We criticize, judge, denigrate, and condemn ourselves repeatedly each day, and then we wonder why we have low self-esteem and do not achieve our goals. Keep your daily journal, record your thoughts, and then look at the results. Psychologists say that most of our emotions are caused by the words that run through our head at any given time. Our mind is like a vacuum; it does not remain empty. If we don't deliberately fill it with positive, constructive words, it will fill itself with our fears, worries, and depressed thoughts.

Once we become aware of what we are saying to ourselves, we must desire to change all those negative dialogues—back to step one. If we truly wish to change and have faith that the Lord will help us, we must change the script of what we are saying to ourselves. We must desire something better for ourselves.

Second, it is important to understand why we have such negative thinking. These automatic thoughts are often programmed early in life. Most parents tend to criticize and correct rather than encourage and praise. As a result, we begin at a very early age to construct internal dialogues like "I cannot do anything right," "I am helpless," "I am ineffective," and so on. All these comments, and many more, decrease our ability to change. When we see ourselves as bad, helpless, or ineffectual, it is difficult to believe that we can achieve goals, become good people, and have success. The problem is that we are still running our lives on scripts that we created as small children. We are no longer who we were conditioned to think we were; maybe we were never that person at all. We condition ourselves for failure.

A good example of this conditioning can be found with elephants at a circus. If you observe the elephants, the biggest and most powerful animals on earth, you will see that they are held with a thin rope tied to a small wooden stake in the ground. If they wanted to, they could tear the stake out with no effort. As soon as the elephants are tied, however, they calm down and remain passive with no attempt to resist or escape. The secret is that when they are young they are chained with a heavy steel chain to an irremovable steel spike sunk deep in the ground. For weeks they fight against the chain, trying to escape until they learn that it is impossible. Then for the rest of their lives all that is necessary is to tie them to a stake and they will not resist because they have been deeply conditioned. Very often, it is the same for us. The words that our parents, peers, and teachers said to us are etched in our mind and condition us years later even though we have grown and changed. Today, we are that adult elephant that can tear the stake out of the ground and achieve all that we desire, but instead we sit passively tied to our past.

> When the subconscious mind must choose between deeply rooted emotions and logic, emotions will almost always win.[8]
>
> —HARV EKER

It is not only what has been said to us as children that shapes us. We are also strongly influenced by the models that our parents set for us. How often as a parent have you said or done things that sound like your father or mother coming out of your past? I once found myself getting angry with my son because he was coughing. He was miserable and had a bad dry cough that just went on and on, and I became increasing irritated until I yelled at him to stop. His hurt expression stopped me, and even I could not understand my anger until I had a flashback. I was five or six years old and on the ski slope with my father in Colorado. I had a clear picture of the mountain, trees, snow, and of my father standing over me yelling at me angrily to stop coughing. I did not understand why he was so angry, and I felt miserable because I just could not stop. I had not thought of that episode for more than thirty years, and there I was yelling at my son just like my father had yelled at me. I apologized immediately and comforted my son, but I was left wondering how this could happen.

If you are trying to be a better spouse or better parent, one of the first ways to change your habits is to examine the models that your parents have imprinted into your thinking. This is true not just for parenting or relationships. Our whole attitude toward money, wealth, and success is rooted in the models that our parents gave us. Until we examine our automatic thoughts, our internal dialogues, and the models that our parents set for us, they will continue to influence us through our life.

> The greatest discovery of my generation is that human beings can alter their lives by altering their attitudes of the mind.[9]
>
> —WILLIAM JAMES

Once we understand that these negative dialogues were inserted into our mind by others, or were created when we were in a different stage of our lives, we need to consciously disassociate ourselves from these thoughts and beliefs. We have to start saying to our subconscious, "This is not me; I do not want to have these thoughts anymore." We start feeling that these beliefs no longer belong to us, and therefore we can consciously choose other beliefs. We can recondition ourselves. This is the last step.

Once we are aware of our dialogues and have some understanding of the conditioning that has taken place and we can disassociate ourselves from those thoughts, we need to recondition ourselves. This means that we must insert into our brain some new positive thoughts and beliefs. Since we are working against years of conditioning, we must do this consciously, deliberately, and repeatedly. Look at some of your negative statements and find a positive affirmation in line with your real capabilities that can replace it. If you find yourself saying, "I cannot do anything right," you could instead say, "I do many things right and I can do this" (thinking or stating what you want to achieve). Or you can say, "I can do all things in the Lord." You must believe in what you are saying, or at least begin to believe it. The affirmation should be short, in the present tense, and positive. Instead of saying, "I will lose a hundred pounds in six months," which probably is not believable and is in the future tense, you should state something like, "I am growing thinner day by day as I follow my plan" or "The less I eat, the more energy I feel." Or, "Sticking to my diet today means a third of a pound lighter for tomorrow." You decide what works for you. Once you have found some positive affirmations that counteract you negative statements, you must repeat them often. Write them down on a 3 x 5 card and put it in your wallet. Each time you take a break during the day, read your affirmations to yourself ten times. It may seem awkward or silly at first, but it is the most effective way to counteract your conditioning. If you want success, you must change your thinking.

There are many books about how to achieve a positive attitude. If you find yourself having problems with your attitude, search for additional information to help you. You cannot achieve success with negative thinking patterns.

ACTION EXERCISES

1. Pick one area of success and start writing down in your notebook all the automatic thoughts that you find yourself thinking on that subject. Write down the internal dialogue that you enact whenever you think of that subject. For example, if you think of wealth and of becoming wealthy, what thoughts start coming to mind—what do you start saying to yourself?
2. Close your eyes, think of that topic, and think back to your childhood. What are the phrases that your parents said to you, or that you heard often, that come to mind? Write down all the statements you can remember hearing from your parents, teachers, peers, or others close to you. For example, what were the normal thoughts, statements, and attitudes made about money in your childhood home?
3. What were the models you had from your parents and others close to you about that same topic? For example, what were their behaviors toward wealth and poverty? Were they rich, poor, insecure?
4. Meditate on the things you have written down. What kind of friend are you to yourself throughout the day? Are these the thoughts, beliefs, and attitudes that you desire to continue using as a model for your own life? If not, disassociate yourself from them. Disown these thoughts.
5. Write down positive thoughts and statements that you truly believe and that reflect the way you wish to start thinking. Start repeating these statements to yourself numerous times each day.
6. Find examples of positive affirmations from the scriptures or other books. Write these down and make them yours by repeating them frequently.

Notes

1. Available from www.saidwhat.co.uk.
2. Available from www.woopit.com.
3. James Allen, *As a Man Thinketh* (Camarillo, CA: DeVorss Pub., 1979).
4. Hal Urban, *Choices That Change Lives*, (New York: Simon & Schuster, 2006), 79.
5. Available from www.thinkexist.com.
6. Available from www.brainyquote.com.
7. Jack D. Hodge, *The Power of Habit* (Bloomington, IN:; 1st Books Library, 2003).
8. Harv Eker, *Secrets of the Millionaire Mind* (New York: Harper Business, 2005), 22.
9. Keller, Jeff Attitude is Everything, Tampa FL INTI Publishing 1999

5 OVERCOME YOUR FEARS

But if ye are prepared, ye shall not fear.
—D&C 38:30

The greatest challenges we will have in trying to reach our goals is not the adversity that comes from without, but our own fears, limiting beliefs, and insecurities that come from within. We create our own handicap because we do not believe we can achieve success. We feel somewhere deep inside us that we are inadequate, or we fear the ridicule of others. You will remember in Dick Lieder's interviews with elderly people that the second biggest regret of people at the end of their lives was that they did not have the courage to live a life with greater purpose and fulfillment. They did not take the risks necessary to obtain success. They were limited by their fears. What about you? No one can obtain the success they seek unless they first face their own fears and insecurities.

There are several fears that hold people back in life. A few of these are the fear of rejection, change, failure or success, and being inadequate. We are social animals, and much of the self-esteem we have comes not from within, but from without. Because we are unsure of ourselves, because we are not sure that we are worthy of love, we depend on others and their judgments to establish whether we are okay. This starts early in life as children seek the approval of their parents. Because parents often only show love when you do something "right," we learn that to have love we must comply. Our insecurities increase as we grow older and peers become our point of reference for our emotional security and self-esteem. There is nothing worse as a teenager than being rejected from the group or being the object of ridicule. Many of us were so deeply wounded by this that to avoid it we learned never to go against the crowd. This then becomes one of the overriding, and often unconscious, rules of our life. Never, ever stand out. Never go against the crowd. Never put yourself in a situation where you might be ridiculed. A Japanese proverb states, "The nail that stands up will be hammered down!" We quickly learn not to stand out.

It is interesting that annual surveys concerning people's greatest fears show that the number one fear is not fear of death or of having cancer or some life threatening disease. The number one fear of Americans is public speaking![1] The fear of getting up in front of others and somehow making a fool of yourself—the fear of ridicule—is more fearsome than a car accident or death. The scriptures give us an excellent example, which, as a psychologist is one of my favorite passages of the scriptures.

Moses was living a quiet life tending the sheep of his father-in-law, Jethro, when on the mountainside he saw a burning bush. He approached it, heard the voice of the Lord, and went closer in awe and reverence. He knew he was in the presence of the Almighty; he took off his shoes and reverently listened to the voice. The Lord told him to go save his people, to go to the pharaoh and tell him to let his people go. Did Moses with fear and trembling say to the Lord, "Of course I'll go, how could I not obey you?" No. He said, "Who am I that I should go unto Pharaoh and that I should bring forth the children of Israel out of Egypt?" (Exodus 3:11).

How many of us ask that same question: Who am I that I can accept this calling? Who am I that the Lord will bless me with prosperity? Who am I that I should become a leader?

The Lord reassured Moses that he was with him and would be at his side, but Moses was not finished. "And Moses said unto God, Behold when I come unto the children of Israel and say unto them, the God of their fathers has sent me unto you; and they say unto me what is his name? What shall I say unto them?" (Exodus 3:13).

Here we start to understand that Moses was not just inquiring to get more information; he was making up excuses, and he wasn't finished yet. The Lord told him his name and reassured him and talked about the covenant his people would make with the Lord. Moses was not satisfied and said, "But behold they will not believe me, nor hearken, unto my voice: for they will say, the Lord hath not appeared unto you" (Exodus 4:1).

Now, put yourself in his place. This is not your home teacher or bishop or even a General Authority calling you to go forth and perform a mission, but God himself. God was calling Moses to perform a mission, and Moses had the audacity to argue with him. The Lord, probably a little frustrated, showed Moses that he would turn Moses' rod into a snake and then back into a rod; his hand would become leprous and then be healed. And if that was not enough, he would turn the water into blood. Moses had not finished, but the real reason for his reluctance to accept this calling came out. Moses finally revealed his deepest fear: "Lord, O Lord I am not eloquent, neither heretofore, nor since thou hast spoken unto thy servant: but I am slow of speech and of a slow tongue" (Exodus 4:10).

There we have it. Moses was afraid. He had a speech defect and was afraid that the people would make fun of him. He was afraid that Pharaoh, and probably even more of his own people, would not accept him and might even ridicule him. He was willing to find excuses with the Lord because of it.

What made Moses great, and what will make the difference in our lives, is that Moses was aware of his fear, but he trusted the Lord and went on to perform his mission despite his fears. By the end of his life, he no longer needed Aaron to talk to his people. Moses had overcome his fear and had become a leader.

This shows us some important steps in overcoming our fears. First we must become aware that we have the fear and that it is our fear that limits our behavior, not other people, society, or fate. We must confess our fear. We must trust in the Lord and find a way to overcome our fear and go out and perform our calling. The Lord provided Aaron as an assistant. Like Moses, we are not always able to complete our assignments on our own. We need to be humble enough to accept help from those close to us.

On a practical level, how often do you know that the best thing you could do for your health is exercise regularly, but you don't do it, in part, because you think you would look ridiculous? Somewhere in your subconscious you are afraid of what the neighbors would think if they saw you waddling down the road, while all the other people who jog are in good shape. On the other hand, you do not go swimming, even though you enjoy it, because you do not look good in a bathing suit.

My father took me skiing for the first time when I was about five or six years old. I remember feeling inadequate because there were three- and four-year-olds who were much better than I was. As a result, I became discouraged and felt that I could never learn. In fact, I never did. I still snowplow my way down the slope. I now grit my teeth at the idea that

I started so young and could have learned so much, but I gave up at five because I was not as good as some four-year-olds. It seems so absurd today, but at five, it was my reality. Unfortunately, this same experience stopped me from learning to skate, to waterski, and to do many other activities that today I would enjoy and that in my youth would have made all the difference in my self-esteem.

Another fear that greatly limits us is the fear of change. A remote tribe in South America is now near extinction. Once anthropologists discovered the tribe deep in the Amazon region, they found that what was once a large, prosperous people had dwindled to a small tribe. They realized that the average life span was very low and few adults lived to be more than forty years old. Gradually the tribe was dying because they were unable to reproduce and raise their children properly to ensure each new generation. In searching for the cause of this unusual mortality rate, the scientists discovered that in the mud the natives used to cover their huts was a parasite that entered their bodies and produced disease, leading to their death. They found that this parasite was native only to this particular region and that by just moving the village thirty miles farther down the river basin, they could avoid this parasite. They explained this to the tribesmen, and the tribe held a council with all the adults and decided that they preferred staying where they were!

All people resist change. It is part of our human nature to want things to stay the same. This story seems absurd to us. Why not just move thirty miles farther down the river? Why die rather than change? However, we are often the same. Some people resist change so vigorously that they would rather die than quit smoking, wear their seat belts and slow down their driving, stop overeating, or change any of those habits that they know are self-destructive. Most of us do things that we know are not good for us, but we do not change.

Success only comes through change, and change starts in our thoughts, our beliefs, and our perceptions. Personal growth requires constant change, and if we allow fear to block us, we cannot improve; we will not reach success.

The fear of change is closely linked to our fear of failure. We do not try anything new because we might make a mistake. Again, this was ingrained in us when we were small children. We were reprimanded when we made mistakes as a child, and for many this meant being yelled at, punished, or even abused. Few parents use the Lord's command to only reprimand when moved upon by the Spirit and then to "show forth an increase of love" toward the child. Not only did our parents punish us for making mistakes, but school was even worse. It is estimated that the average child will take over eight thousand tests, quizzes, and exams in his scholastic career. The whole purpose of a test is to reward those who make the fewest mistakes. As a result, we learn that making a mistake is equivalent to failure. So, in order not to feel the bad emotions associated with being a failure, we avoid any situation where we might make mistakes or fail.

This means that we only feel comfortable in doing things we know we are capable of performing. It means that when we do make a mistake, we justify ourselves by blaming others or the circumstances to show that it was not our fault. In the end, we never try anything new; we never challenge ourselves because we might fail. This is what the experts call staying in your comfort zone—doing what you know you can do and avoiding everything else. This, however, will never let you reach your goals or have success in this life or in eternal life. Eternal life means progress, and progress requires growth and change. Growth means we are going to make mistakes and probably fail many times along the way.

Something we were withholding
Made us weak—
Until we learned
It was ourselves we were withholding
From this land of living—
And Thenceforth
Found Salvation
In Surrender[2]

—ROBERT FROST

What activities are you giving up because you are afraid that you may fail? Some people unconsciously sabotage themselves on the job because they are afraid that if promoted they will not be able to handle the responsibilities. Maybe they do not feel confident in making presentations or taking responsibility or some other aspect of the job. What are your greatest fears, and how are they holding you back from success in your life? You have to face the fear, confess the fear, and, above all, change your attitude and see failure as just an opportunity.

The classic example of this is Thomas Edison, who is considered the greatest inventor of all time. He invented over 1,300 different patented items, many of which have changed our lives. When he invented the light bulb, he tried out almost 10,000 different metals and substances before he found that tungsten would withstand the intense heat and illuminate the bulb. This means that he made almost 10,000 mistakes, or failed almost 10,000 times. But he did not see it this way. Edison merely stated that he discarded 10,000 options before he found the right one.

When you are committed to success, you are also committed to leaving your comfort zone and trying new things. It has been said that the definition of insanity is doing the same thing over and over but expecting a different result. Many of us do just that. We try one diet after another, we get discouraged, we quit, and then we start all over again with a different diet, expecting that somehow something will change. On the other hand, we continue spending our money the same way, running up debts, trying to pay them off, working harder, getting more stressed, shopping to relieve the stress, and accumulating more debt. It just does not work. If you want different results, you must change what you are doing. If you want success, you have to face your fears and leave the your comfort zone.

The road to success has many tempting parking spaces.[3]

—STEVE POTTER

The fear of not being capable of facing life's challenges is perhaps underlying all of our fears. We feel inadequate. Deep inside we feel that other people know what they are doing but that we do not and someone will discover our secret. The truth is that everyone has the same fear. We must learn to face life with courage. I am sure that Nephi was quite afraid as he stood before Laban to obtain the plates and as he had to flee with his brothers to escape death. Abinadi could not help but be afraid as he faced the flames for his beliefs. Daniel faced the wrath of the king repeatedly as he held true to his principles, even to be thrown in the lion's den. He did not surrender to his fears. Joseph Smith went from one threat to another and finally gave his life. All men of God face their fear, trust in the Lord, and go forward and do God's will.

Jonah is the exception. He was called to go to Nineveh, a city of great sin and idolatry, to preach repentance to the inhabitants. He was so afraid that he ran away and tried to hide from the Lord. It took three days in a whale's belly to finally realize that there are worse things than what we fear. Many of us hide our fears from the Lord and from ourselves.

Facing your fears takes courage. Winston Churchill once said, "Courage is rightly considered the foremost of the virtues, for upon it, all others depend."[4] Courage is the quality of leaders. It is the quality of men and women of success. It is interesting that on the Serengeti plains of Africa, naturalists have discovered an easy way to determine which animal is the leader of the herd. When a predator such as a lion or hyena approaches a herd of grazing animals, the animals will pick up the scent and start drifting away in the opposite direction. The leader of the herd will then place himself between the herd and the danger, risking his own life to buy time for the rest of the herd. The leader always "turns toward danger."[5] As Mark Twain said, "Courage is not the lack of fear or absence of fear. It is the mastery of fear; control of fear."[6] If we want to succeed in life, we must turn toward the danger. We must face our personal fears, admit them, and then trust in the Lord. We must launch ourselves in the direction of our goals. For this reason, faith is at the base of our progress. We must have faith that the Lord will sustain our efforts.

If you do not do the thing you fear, the fear controls your life.[7]

—GLENN FORD

Dr. Robert Ronstadt, a business instructor at Babson College, did an interesting study. For twelve years he studied all the graduates of the business school who went on to establish a business of their own. Some built successful businesses, but many failed in their endeavors. Ronstadt found that the one quality that distinguished those who founded prosperous activities was that they had the courage to launch their business with no guarantees of success. They were willing to risk failure in the pursuit of their dreams. He called this the "corridor principle." It states that when you take the first steps toward your goal, you begin to move down a corridor of time. As you move down the corridor, doors of opportunity will open on either side of you. You are able to see these opportunities, however, only if you have already entered the corridor. They are hidden to those who remain stationary at the entrance. Those who never venture forth never see the opportunities. We must first leap with faith.[8]

> The difference between average and successful people is that successful people do not waste time arguing for their limitations, they transcend them.
> —M. SCOTT PECK

Courage takes faith. Are you willing to overcome your fears to achieve your dreams?

ACTION EXERCISES

1. Meditate on what your fears are and write them down. Think about whether these fears are real or just the result of past conditioning. Write down your considerations.
2. Deal with your fears one at a time and make a firm commitment to overcome them. Think about and write down a strategy to overcome each fear.
3. Read the story of your favorite prophet and examine all the ways that he used courage in his life to follow God's will.
4. Face your fear. Act as if you had no fear and write down the results. Try it for a day, two days, a week, and a month until it becomes a habit.

Notes

1. Susan Jeffers, *Feel the Fear and Do It Anyway*, (New York: Fawcett Columbine, 1987).
2. Robert Frost, "The Gift Outright."
3. Steve Potter, *Thoughts from a Southpaw.*
4. Brian Tracy, *Change Your Thinking Change Your Life* (New Jersey: John Wiley & Sons, Inc., 2003), 237.
5. Ibid., 239.
6. Ibid., 240.
7. Ibid.
8. Ibid., p 241
9. M. Scott Peck, *The Road Less Traveled* (New York: Simon & Schuster, 1978).

STEP 2

PREPARE YOURSELF

Now that you have examined your dreams and have decided to follow them with faith and commitment, you must begin to prepare your action plan. You have begun the process of changing yourself by examining your thoughts and attitudes and facing your fears. You are now ready to move to the next level. You must prepare yourself for your success.

There are four steps to your preparation. All success comes from a realistic evaluation of your strengths and weaknesses. Your weaknesses are the weights that keep you down, and your strengths are the helium in your balloon that allows you to soar. You must develop your talents. All the success you will have in life will depend on the talents and capacities that you develop.

Next, you must prepare yourself. You must read, take courses, obtain new knowledge, find help from mentors and experienced people, and develop new insights and strategies. To reach any goal you must prepare yourself diligently.

You must establish realistic goals that are specific, timely, and obtainable. Goals are the rudder that keeps you headed in the right direction. Finally, you must establish an action plan to reach those goals. You must have a written plan with a schedule that you can use to evaluate your progress. These are the four steps of preparation.

THE STEPS TO SUCCESS

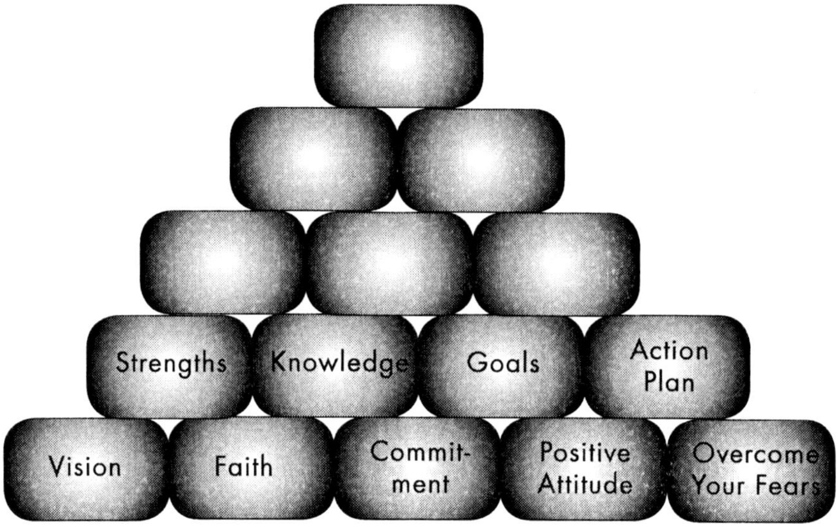

6 STRENGTHS

And all this for the benefit of the church of the living God, that every man may improve upon his talent, that every man may gain other talents, yea, even a hundred fold.
—D&C 82:18

There are two important laws of the universe: (1) you will never rise above your greatest weakness, and (2) you will only excel with your greatest strength.

One of the reasons that we do not achieve all that we could is that we have not properly evaluated our strengths and weaknesses. The Lord has asked that we overcome our weaknesses. In Ether 12:27 the Lord states: "And if men come unto me I will show them their weaknesses. I give unto men weakness that they may be humble; and my grace is sufficient for all men that humble themselves before me, and have faith in me, then I will make weak things become strong unto them." Turning our weaknesses into strengths can take our entire life as we attempt to identify and overcome these weaknesses. But a person who concentrates only on their weaknesses will quickly become discouraged and will not succeed. We must also become aware of the special gifts and talents we possess and use and develop these to bless others. It is our talents that will determine our success, not our weaknesses. It is through our strong points that we must overcome all obstacles. Anyone who tries to succeed using someone else's method or gift is doomed to failure.

I particularly like the Old Testament because the people, prophets, and men of God are so real and have so many faults. King David is an excellent example of the two laws. David is not our usual man of God, solemn and sober. He is joyful, full of life. He sings; he dances in the streets; he loves life. He composes the Psalms with a heart full of gratitude to the Lord. He has great faith in the Lord and respect for others. He is able to form deep relationships with others, including the legendary friendship with Jonathan because he is full of love. Because he loves life and loves people, his people in turn adore him. His soldiers are faithful to him even unto death; the population is loyal to him. If he had given up his nature, had been dour and solemn in becoming a king, do you believe that he would have achieved all he did in uniting all Israel under one kingdom and defeating his enemies? In the same way, it was his love of life and people, and particularly women, that became his downfall. He did not overcome his greatest weakness, and he suffered for it.

God has given each of us our "marching orders." Our purpose here on earth is to find those orders and carry them out. Those orders acknowledge our special gifts.[1]

—SOREN KIERKEGAARD

When we seek success in any area of life, we will succeed through our talents. This is what God has given us to bless the world. If we are not using our strengths, if we have never identified our gifts, we will not have much success. If I want to become a better parent, I can certainly try to emulate other good parents who I know, and if I have failings I should work on overcoming them. But I will not become a great parent unless I use those natural talents that God has bestowed on me. It is through our passions and interests that we can transmit love to our children. After reading many of his books, I personally tried for a time, to be a father like Stephen Covey, who comes up with fantastic creative activities for his family. But it just isn't in me. It does not work for me because I am not Stephen Covey. I have other talents. I have a passion for basketball and sports, and I still play with my children every Saturday. I love nature and the mountains, and we take yearly vacations where I can transmit this love. I am a good listener, and I strive to use this talent to stay close to my children. My successes as a father and what I will leave in the hearts of my children will be proportional to those positive qualities that I possess; it does not come from trying to do it according to someone else. Of course this is also why it is good to have two parents and maybe even grandparents and relatives involved in my children's lives so that they can compensate where I have no passion. My greatest success as a parent will always be in those areas where I excel. On the other hand, if I were to have a big problem with keeping my temper, I would need to work on that to make it a strength, because otherwise it could ruin all that I do with my positive qualities.

The same is true for any project. If you want to lose weight, do not make it a struggle of self-discipline. Instead, start thinking of how to use your strengths to overcome your obstacles. How can you change your lifestyle using your talents? Maybe you enjoy nature and can start gardening. Maybe you are very friendly and could start a self-help group. Maybe still you are very generous and could cook at a shelter for the poor rather than cook so much for your family. It does not matter what qualities you have; if you can identify them, you can use them for success. If you do not, you will fail again. Just because many people jog to stay healthy does not mean that it will work for you if you hate jogging.

> The person born with a talent they are meant to use will find their greatest happiness in using it.[2]
>
> —JOHANN WOLFGANG VON GOETHE

None of the prophets were the same. All were very different people who developed different talents and used those talents to bless the world. Nephi was a builder. Moroni was a great general and leader. Daniel showed great faith and courage as he entered the lion's den. Isaiah and Matthew were intellectuals who delighted in studying the scriptures. Peter was spontaneous and impulsive. John was reverent and sincere, and Paul had great knowledge and culture. All of these men of God had different characters and different talents, and it was by the use of their talents that they became great. There is not just one correct model for everyone. You should not strive to be a different person; instead, you should strive to develop what is uniquely you. You were sent on this earth with your inherent qualities to better this world. You should strive to be more like you. At the same time, we remember that we can never rise above our greatest weaknesses, so the more we can improve our weaknesses the higher we can rise. But it is our strengths that make us unique.

> We are here to be excited from youth to old age, to have insatiable curiosity about the world. . . . We are here also to help others by practicing a friendly attitude. And every person is born for a purpose. Everyone has a God-given potential, in essence built into them. And if we are to live life to its fullest, we must realize that potential.[3]
>
> —NORMAN VINCENT PEALE

How do we identify our talents and strengths? What comes to you naturally? What do you like to do if you have a choice? What are you passionate about? When you study or work, how do you approach it? Are you well organized? Are you creative? Are you introverted or extroverted? Do you like being with people or do you prefer being alone? Are you thoughtful or are you impulsive? Do people come to you with their problems? Why or why not? Do others come to you to help them organize a party or a luncheon? These and many other questions can help you identify your strengths and passions. There are many books about how to find your positive qualities, and there are tests you can take. You should meditate on your life and find what works for you, because that will be your path to success in all of your endeavors. In the book *Soar with Your Strengths,* the authors give five ways to identify your strengths:

1. Listen to your yearnings—Yearnings are most often triggered when you see a performance and you say to yourself, "I'd like to do that; or I'd like to try that."
2. Watch for satisfaction—Those activities that give you the greatest satisfaction most often relate to your strong points and talents.
3. Watch for rapid learning—Those activities that you seem to pick up with no effort, that just come to you naturally are your innate talents.
4. Glimpses of excellence—When you perform a task and find that you can do it better than others, then there is true excellence in what you are doing. Somehow it relates to your strengths.
5. Total performance of excellence—When the task or activity that you perform remains excellent in all aspects, you have the confirmation that you are using your inner gifts.[4]

As an example, I am well organized, and I can help others keep things in order. I have a lot of personal initiative; I have many ideas and am good at starting a project. But I am terrible at continuing anything. I lose interest in a project that lasts longer than a few weeks. I do not follow through well. Therefore, thinking about just one area, I can come up with ideas for twenty books. I can begin the project, but when it starts getting difficult and there are so many chapters to write, I get bogged down. I have had to learn to attack the project from various angles. When I start slowing down in writing, I stop and start a new project of searching for all the citations. When I get tired of that, I sometimes start from the last chapter first to see how I want to end it, and so on, until I am able to complete the entire project. I can use my strong points to come up with new ideas and overcome my weak points by searching out different strategies. Until I was aware of these strengths and weaknesses, however, I would just try to trudge on and would get more depressed and never finish the project. The same was true, of course, for the decades of dieting. No diet lasted more than a few weeks, and the end result was more pounds rather than less. Knowing myself better, I can find new strategies for success. In this case I have used my passion for basketball and for being with my children to increase my activity level and change my lifestyle.

When I think of someone who developed his talents, Joseph Smith comes to mind. Here we have a young man with just a few years of schooling who, in his brief life, learned German and Hebrew, not to mention reformed Egyptian. He became a biblical authority and established the school of prophets to teach and learn spiritual and temporal doctrines. He learned to think deeply about spiritual concepts and wrote and expressed them to others. What most impresses me, however, was his talent for gaining trust and loyalty. As a young boy of fourteen, he went home to his parents and siblings and told them of his experience in the Sacred Grove and they believed him. Anyone who has had children knows that older brothers never believe younger brothers, yet his brothers believed him and were faithful to him even to their deaths. Joseph established the Church when he was in his twenties. He was recognized by others—young and old, learned and unlearned—as a prophet of the Lord. They followed him into the wilderness and established cities and elected him as their mayor.

I have difficulty coming up with anyone else who has gained such loyalty and trust at such a young age. Think of the leadership qualities that Joseph developed in his brief life. He was indeed the prophet who could restore the gospel in this last dispensation.

What are the qualities that will make you a success? Whether on the job, at home as a spouse and parent, in your church duty, or in your personal life, what are the strengths you will need to succeed?

Make a list of them here:

1.
2.
3.
4.
5.
6.
7.
8.
9.
10.

What are your greatest weaknesses that limit you?

1.
2.
3.

If you find that you can think of ten weaknesses but only three strengths, join the club. This, however, will not help you. You need to concentrate on your positive qualities not your weaknesses.

What qualities do you possess on the job that you can capitalize on to get ahead? Identify the strengths you have and see how you can apply them to your job. If there is very little convergence of your talents and the job you do, you may wish to consider a job that is aligned with your talents and yearnings. Just plugging along, even with diligence, does not lead to success. Success is obtained by using those unique qualities that we have to make a difference. All great men have achieved excellence through their special talents. You must discover yours.

ACTION EXERCISES

1. List the activities that give you the most enjoyment. What skills are you using?
2. What skills come most easily to you? In what do you seem naturally endowed?
3. What are your passions? What would you do with your free time?

What would you do even if you were not paid or rewarded?

4. Write down all the skills and passions that you can think of. Now evaluate how much of your time and energy you dedicate to improving these skills.
5. Write down how you can use these skills to become a better parent, spouse, person, and worker. How can you use your strengths to improve your life and the lives of others near you?
6. What is your greatest weakness? How does it keep you humble? What strategy can you use to improve it? Do you have faith that the Lord will help you make it a strong point?
7. Write down a strategy to improve your weakness, and begin today.

Notes

1. Janet Bray and Chris Attwood, *The Passion Test, Fairfield* (IO Enlightened Alliances, LLC ,2006), 15.
2. Ibid., 31.
3. Brian D. Biro, *Beyond Success* (Hamilton, MT: Pygmalion Press, 1995), 155.
4. Donald Clifton and Paula Nelson, *Soar with Your Strengths* (New York: Dell Publishing Group, Inc., 1992).

7 KNOWLEDGE

Seek ye diligently and teach one another words of wisdom; yea, seek ye out of the best books words of wisdom; seek learning, even by study and also by faith.

—D&C 88:118

It has been said that five years from now you will be exactly as you are now, do what you are still doing, and think the same thoughts as you think now, except you will expose yourself to different things. That is, you will be the same person you are today except for the books you read, the people you meet, the new experiences you try, and the input you receive from the media, particularly TV and movies. If you wish to progress and grow, not only do you need to seek out new experiences, but you need to look at the quality of those new experiences.

Successful people are chronic learners. As Brian Tracy states, "Leaders are readers."[1] One study shows that the top 10 percent of earners in America spend at least two hours a day reading specialized journals, books, or articles that will enhance their job-related knowledge. They have learned that specialized knowledge is the key to success. On the other hand, a survey by the American Booksellers Association found that 80 percent of American families did not buy a single book in the last year. Not only that, but they found that 58 percent of Americans never read another book after they leave school, including 42 percent of college graduates. Successful people not only read, but they spend their time in the car listening to audio books, and they attend conferences and seminars that can enhance their learning and their careers. They are hungry for knowledge. Knowledge is what provides the new perspectives that can change our lives.

"The mind is like a parachute—it only works when it is open."[2]
BRIAN D. BIRO

There is a celestial principle that states that God will never do for us what we can do for ourselves. When we reach our limits, the Lord will provide, but only if we have done everything humanly possible. In this day in which the Lord has poured out his Spirit on the earth and the volume of new knowledge is doubling every year, we must do our part to investigate the available knowledge. How many parents pray to the Lord asking for help to resolve their problems with their children but have never read a book or attended a class where the answer might be available? Is the Lord going to come down and reveal to them what he has already revealed to others? No, this goes against celestial laws. The same is true for our marital relationships, our careers, and the many problems that we encounter in our lives. Almost invariably, the answer is available, but we have to do the work to seek it out. Doctrine and Covenants section 9 is very clear about how we receive revelation: "Behold, you have not understood; you have supposed that I would give it unto you, when you took no thought save it was to ask me. But, behold, I say unto you, that you must first study it out in your mind; then you must ask me if it be right, and if it is right I will cause that your bosom shall burn within you; therefore you shall feel that it is right" (vv. 7–8).

The Lord has counseled us to seek out the best books, to increase our knowledge both of gospel principles and of scientific and worldly knowledge. In D&C 88 he says:

> Teach ye diligently and my grace shall attend you, that ye may be instructed more perfectly in theory, in principle, in doctrine, in the law of the gospel, in all things that pertain unto the kingdom of God, that are expedient for you to understand; Of things, both in heaven and in the earth, and under the earth; things which have been, things which are, things which must shortly come to pass; things which are at home, things which are abroad; the wars and perplexities of nations, and the judgments which are on the land; and a knowledge also of countries and of kingdoms—That ye may be prepared in all things when I shall send you again to magnify the calling whereunto I have called you.

Leaders are readers. Are you? If you desire success, whether spiritual or temporal, you need to change your habits to include reading. Remember too that the Lord says to read good books. Books can help you increase your knowledge and stimulate your thoughts, but there are also trashy books and magazines that can depress your spirits and taint your thoughts. Which do you read? You must eliminate the trash, or in five years you will be less than what you are today. You must find ways to increase your knowledge. Today there are audio books that you can listen to in your car while you drive. There are courses, conferences, and seminars on almost every topic. There are self-help groups where you can exchange information, ideas, and problems with others who are trying to better themselves. The Internet is a fabulous source of information and contacts. There is information on any subject you can imagine, and there are people willing to share their experiences with you who are just a click of the mouse away. If you do not have a computer or do not know how to use the Internet, remember that progress is all about change.

Books, magazines, and other forms of the written word are important sources of new ideas, new perceptions, and new beliefs. But they are not the only sources. Many people obtain most of their stimulation, new ideas, and new perspectives from the people with whom they associate. Other people, particularly friends and family, are often our greatest source of emotional support and stimulation, and all progress must involve those closest to us. It is true, however, that we tend to associate with people who share our interests and ideas and who think much like we do. Are the people you associate with stimulating? Do they give you different perspectives on issues? When was the last time you felt inspired to do something after talking to one of your friends? Usually, we choose our friends because we are comfortable with them, because they reinforce our values and beliefs. This, however, often leads to what is called "groupthink" in which a whole group of people shares similar beliefs and attitudes. Because they think alike, they mutually reinforce the idea that theirs is the only right belief, and they are no longer open to other options. We are stimulated to think and reevaluate our perceptions and beliefs when we associate with people who are very different from ourselves. You must be open to new possibilities and new ideas. Therefore, make a resolution to make friends or at least associate with someone new who is very different from you in age, education, upbringing, culture, race, or some other aspect. Seek out different ideas instead of seeking to confirm what you already believe.

> You can't fly with the eagles if you continue to scratch with the turkeys.[3]
> —ZIG ZIGLAR

Seek out people who have already succeeded in the endeavor you are undertaking and find out how they did it. Then use them as your role model. Dr. David McClelland of Harvard found that 95 percent of the success you will have in life is determined by your reference group. These are the people that you usually associate with, compare yourself to, and consider to be your in-crowd. They are the people you consider to be like you. If, however, you wish to change, if you wish to grow, your reference group must change. If you remain with the same associates and they aren't growing too, they will hold you back in your progress.[4] Several authors advise that if you want to be a millionaire, one of the first steps is to start associating with millionaires. Learn who they are, how they act, what they think, how they prepare themselves. They will then become your reference group, and you will start imitating their behavior. If you continue associating with negative, superficial, or indolent people, then that is who you will remain. The same is true if you want to become a better parent. Pick out people who are particularly good with their children. Start associating with them; observe their listening habits, their interaction, and their attitudes toward their children. If you wish to become a man of God, associate with other spiritual giants and follow their example. Just by associating with them you will begin to absorb their mentality and be stimulated to emulate their behaviors.

> A single conversation with a wise man is better than ten years of study.[5]
> —CHINESE PROVERB

Because people are such an important source of stimulation and change, you have to be very selective in the people with whom you associate. They can change you for the good or the bad. Beware of people who are negative, who always complain and judge others. Beware of gossip and people who talk behind others' backs. Beware of people who are full of prejudice and are small-minded. All of these people bring a negative attitude that is contagious. They dampen your spirits, dull your mind, and try to involve you with their small view of the world. These are people who live in fear and who try to pull people down to their level. Stay away from them, avoid them, or at least be aware of what they are doing and do not participate. Seek out people who are positive, people who are striving for excellence. The Lord says again in D&C 130 that the same associations we have here we will continue in the next life. "And that same sociality which exists among us here will exist among us there, only it will be coupled with eternal glory" (v. 2). You need to seek out celestial people and associate with them.

President Thomas S. Monson said, "Essential to your success and happiness is the advice 'Choose your friends with caution.' We tend to become like those whom we admire, and they are usually our friends. We should associate with those who, like us, are planning not for temporary convenience, shallow goals, or narrow ambition—but rather with those who value the things that matter most, even eternal objectives."[6]

There is nothing so mind numbing, depressing, and wasteful as modern TV. I know—I have been assiduously watching it for years! When I was young, my mother decided that we would be better off without TV. I have to thank her because, as a result, I developed a love for reading, but at the same time, growing up I felt constantly left out, as other children would talk about their favorite TV shows. Consequently, as an adult, for the next thirty years, I would keep up on all the shows, sitcoms, and sports until I finally realized that 90 percent of what I was watching I really didn't enjoy. The moral of the story? Moderation in all things. There are good shows, but in general very little that most people watch on TV greatly enhances their lives.

Elder M. Russell Ballard commented on the dangers of watching too much television:

> The fall of the year is when television airs its season premieres and introduces its new shows. A friend told me that there are 37 new TV series being inaugurated this fall. As he has read the reviews, he has found few if any of them that he would want his children to watch. Most of the sitcoms, dramas, and reality shows contain immorality, violence, and subtle ridicule of traditional values and traditional families. Each year the new shows seem to get worse, pushing the envelope of what the public will accept. What comes out of Hollywood, off the Internet, and in much of today's music creates a web of decadence that can trap our children and endanger all of us.[7]

Some interesting studies have found that excessive TV viewing is similar to any other type of addiction. People watch TV to relax, but the more they watch, the more depressed they become. Most people spend much more time than they would like in front of the TV, but they cannot tear themselves away. People also go through withdrawal symptoms when they are deprived of TV, similar to any drug addict.[8] The real question is, are you enhancing your mind and stimulating new thoughts and ideas, or are you avoiding thinking at all and numbing your mind? Are you filling your mind with positive attitudes and beliefs, or just feeling empty and depressed? Is the TV making you a better person, or could you use your time more purposefully to achieve your goals, including just going to bed and resting? There is probably no other media where the old computer adage is more appropriate: "Garbage in, garbage out." If you fill your mind with garbage, you can only get garbage out.

It has been said that the difference between a rich man and a poor man is how they spend their free time. How do you spend yours? Look at your life and habits critically and ask yourself, am I gaining the knowledge I need to obtain the success I want? Am I associating with the people that will help me and stimulate me to meet my goals? Am I using my time wisely to become the best person possible? Do I seek out and accept new ideas, new perspectives, and new experiences, or do I just want to remain comfortable? Five years from now, will I be a better person than I am now because I have created positive things in my mind and my life, or will I still be in the same spot? Am I on my way to the celestial kingdom, or am I still in my comfort zone? The choice is yours.

ACTION EXERCISES

1. Read the scriptures every day.
2. Make a list of books that you would like to read. Start the first book today.
3. Examine your circle of friends and acquaintances. Who are the most negative people in your group? How much time do you spend with them? How could you reduce this time together?
4. Are there people you know who are very different from you? How could get to know them better?
5. Schedule your TV time during the week, and carefully select only the programs you really want to watch.

6. Find out if there are courses or online courses at your local community college that you could take to improve your talents and knowledge.
7. Buy some audio books and start listening to them.

Notes

1. Brian Tracy, *Million Dollar Habits* (Canada: Entrepreneur Press, 2004), 56.
2. Brian D. Biro, *Beyond Success* (Hamilton, Montana: Pygmalion Press, 1995), 79.
3. Harv Eker, *Secrets of the Millionaire Mind* (New York: Harper Business, 2005), 62.
4. David McClelland, *The Achieving Society* (Van Nostrand, 1961).
5. Hal Urban, *Choices That Change Lives* (New York: Simon & Schuster, 2006).
6. Thomas S. Monson, "Be Thou an Example," *Ensign*, Apr. 2005.
7. M. Russell Ballard, "Let Our Voices Be Heard," *Ensign*, Nov. 2003, 16.
8. R. Kubley R. and M. Csikszsentmihalyi, "Television Addiction Is No Mere Metaphor," *Scientific American*, 2003

8 GOALS

For behold, this is my work and my glory—to bring to pass the immortality and eternal life of man.

—MOSES 1:39

The Lord has always had a clear goal for his work. He knows exactly what he wants to achieve. Do you have goals that are just as clear?

> The man who succeeds above his fellows is the one who early in life clearly discerns his object, and toward that object habitually directs his powers.[1]
>
> —EDWARD BULWER-LYTTON

There are literally hundreds of books on the market that explain why goals should be made, how they should be made, and how to evaluate them. And still most people do not have clear, usable goals.

One study found that 92 percent of people make New Year's resolutions, but only 40 percent attain any of the resolutions they make. And most people are not even sure what their resolutions were last year.[2] Are you?

Why did I have a New Year's resolution for twenty years to lose weight and never succeed to lose it? What goes wrong with the process? What are some of the steps we should remember?

The first step in setting goals is to formulate exactly what we want to achieve and then write it down. An interesting study done at Harvard University found that when the graduating seniors of the class of 1962 were asked their life goals, only 60 percent could clearly state any goals that they had, and only 5 percent had written them down. In a followup survey twenty years later, those 5 percent were the only ones who had reached their goals. In addition, those 5 percent had out-earned the other 95 percent combined. It is estimated that only 3 percent of the population have specific goals for their lives. It is also found that the most successful people in society are always among those 3 percent.[3] So, follow the path of other successful people and write down your goals.

You should start with long-term goals—what you want to achieve in the next five to ten years. Then specify how you will obtain those goals by breaking them into yearly, monthly, and daily goals. Some authors suggest that we differentiate between general or overriding goals that set the course that we want to take and performance goals that specify what actions we need to take.

You need to establish your priorities. Many people have specific goals for work but have never established any goals for their marriage or their family life. You will only accomplish what you clearly envision and make part of your dominant thinking. If you want a celestial marriage or a celestial family, you will not obtain them by chance. You must channel your energies toward achieving specific goals that you have established. Many people never set goals in the areas of their lives that have the highest priority, and then they wonder why they did not succeed. You should also prioritize your goals within each area of life. You should not waste your time working on goals that make little difference to your progress. For each area of your life, you should ask yourself, what one behavior, if I were to change it, would make the most difference in my life? Then establish a goal to change that behavior or acquire a new behavior or habit. Let me repeat that because it is perhaps the most important question of this book. **What one behavior, if you were to change it, would make the most difference in your life?**

Once you reach your intermediate goals, you should quickly set new goals. You are never too old to look ahead at what you need to accomplish next. This is a life of constant growth and progress. Elder Marvin Ashton said:

> It has been said by Bruce Barton that, "When we're through changing, we're through." There is no age when we are too old or too young or just too middle-aged to change. Perhaps old age really comes when a person finally gives up the right, challenge, and joy of changing. We should remain teachable. How easy it is to become set. We must be willing to establish goals whether we are sixty, seventy, fifty, or fifteen. Maintain a zest for life. Never should there be a time when we are unwilling to improve ourselves through meaningful change.[4]

In his book *The 10 Natural Laws of Successful Time Management,* Hyrum Smith Jr. advises that goals should follow the SMART formula. They should be specific, measurable, action-oriented, realistic, and timely.[5]

Specific—Most people do not obtain their goals because their goals are not specific or measurable. You could set a goal to be healthier. But what does that mean? At the end of the year, how will you know whether you have achieved it? It may be a good general goal that sets the course that you want to achieve, but you need something more specific to work with. The same is true for goals such as becoming a better parent, having success on the job, or becoming more humble. None of these will lead to an action plan. We must focus on a specific behavior or behaviors that we have identified and want to change. For your five-year goal, you can write "be healthier," but for your performance goals, you must identify specific behaviors you wish to change. An example would be "I will eat two portions of fresh fruit every day and will take a twenty-minute walk three times a week. I will limit fast food meals to once a week and have a biannual medical checkup." These are specific, they lead to our overall goal of being healthier, and we can measure them and evaluate our progress. In the same way, if being a better parent is the general direction in which we want to move, we must identify specific behaviors that will take us there. It might be that at the end of every day I want to have expressed or have shown my children three times more positive affirmations than negative commands or criticisms, or I want to have at least forty-five minutes of quality interaction and fun play with each child every day. Again, these are specific and measurable. On the job we may want more success, but what are the behaviors that will allow this to happen? If you are a salesman, you can quantify the number of cold calls that you will make every day, or you can have specific goals like arriving fifteen minutes earlier each day to start your day more efficiently. How do we become more humble? What are some of the specific behaviors that make up humility? Before we can create performance goals, the first step is always to find the particular behaviors that must change. Maybe your performance goal would be to begin a gratitude journal in which you write down all the events and things that you are grateful for. Or you could write what you appreciate in each person you meet so that you can better see the good qualities in others. You could reduce your complaining in half. When you change these behaviors, you will know you have come closer to being humble.

Measurable—When we want to change a behavior, it is often a good policy to first establish a baseline of measurements. It is easy if my goal is just to lose weight. I can measure it at the beginning, and then take measurements at regular intervals to evaluate my progress. But if I want to change my behavior so my children will stop fighting so much, how do I really know how often they are fighting? It can be very revealing just to observe that behavior and chart it. Often we overestimate the frequency of behavior, particularly when it is other people's behavior, and we underestimate the frequency of our own. I can't stop swearing overnight. I should be able to chart it just like I would weight loss, but most people never even create a baseline. They never actually chart how often they are performing that behavior, so they never really know if they are improving or not. You must measure your behavior in some way or you will never know if you are reaching your goal. If you are just not aware of your behaviors, enlist some other family member to measure and chart your progress. Usually, they will be very happy to help.

Action-oriented—Your goals should focus on behaviors to perform rather than internal qualities. Even if my goal is to improve an internal quality like friendliness or courage, I have to break this down into specific behaviors that I desire to acquire or to terminate; otherwise, I will never be able to make the goal specific or measurable.

Realistic—Besides not having specific, measurable goals, the other pitfall most of us fall into is not making our goals very realistic. Even though it has taken me twenty years to put on eighty extra pounds, I want to lose them all this year—in fact, in the next six months. This is not realistic and is therefore not attainable. And even worse, it works against the overall goal of good health to lose weight that rapidly. Likewise, people set goals to be a millionaire in three years when they are making currently making thirty thousand dollars a year, or they want the perfect marriage tomorrow. Be optimistic in your goals, and challenge yourself to succeed. But when goals are too unrealistic, we only become discouraged. There will be difficulties, delays, and failures along the way. The better we can incorporate this into our plan by being realistic in the beginning, the easier it is to obtain the goal. The question you should ask is, is the goal practical? Is it within reason? Is it possible? If the answer is to each of these questions is yes, then go ahead and break the goal down into small pieces that you can achieve day by day.

All goals should have a timetable. This too should be specific. Leaving things vague leaves no room for comparison and evaluation. You should know on any given day what you need to do that day to obtain your goal and how you are doing on your timetable. You should always break goals down into small pieces that you can handle day by day. Large projects should be broken down into manageable bites. If I am a student taking several courses and have five 800-page textbooks read, study, and digest in 16 weeks, I know that each week I have to study and digest 250 pages. Therefore, I need to digest 50 pages a day, except on weekends. The task that initially seems overwhelming becomes more manageable, and every day I know what I need to do to reach my goal.

President Howard W. Hunter said,

> Whenever we tackle a gospel imperative, immediate goals will help us master it. Our decision to read scripture becomes quite practical when we decide to read a chapter at night before we go to sleep. We should set up long-range and eternal goals, to be sure they will be the guides and inspiration of a lifetime; but we should not forget the countless little immediate objectives to be won tomorrow and tomorrow and tomorrow. To win and pass these objectives marks our progress toward the greater goals and ensures happiness and the feelings of success along the way.[6]

Having a timetable gives more urgency to achieving the goal; it challenges you to make the daily changes that are necessary to achieve what you want. I may set out to be more meek and humble by the end of my life, but if I do not break this down into specific behaviors that I can work on, and if I do not set a timetable for achieving each of these behaviors, where will I be at the end of my life?

Because your goals are measurable and have a timetable, you can now make periodic evaluations. Where are you on your timetable? How close are you to your goal? This is important because in any achievement there will be setbacks. You need to ask yourself, why am I having this difficulty? Was my goal realistic? Was my timetable realistic? Were there other factors that I didn't consider? This allows you to make midcourse corrections or to redefine what you need to do.

Brother Ashton states:

> In conclusion let me suggest that each of us conduct a personal interview with ourselves periodically to see how well we are doing. To make this most meaningful we need to have challenging goals for ourselves that require us to stretch ourselves in order to attain them. Let us be truly objective with ourselves as we conduct these personal interviews. Some of the best planning and supervision that any of us can take part in is the planning and supervision that we do for ourselves as we take definite steps to chart a meaningful course in life by establishing goals

> and methods for reaching them and then checking up on ourselves. In doing so we should let the gospel of Jesus Christ be our guide, and use the measuring sticks that the Lord himself, and his prophets—including our living prophets today—have given for our guidance.[7]

Finally, you need to reward yourself. Too often we make achieving goals all work and no fun. Build in rewards as you achieve different milestones along the way. After losing ten pounds, buy a new dress. After fifty pounds, buy a completely new wardrobe!

The reason that most people do not write down their goals, make them specific, and even attempt to measure them or set a timetable is that they are afraid of failure. Fear of failure is the overriding reason people prefer to stay in their comfort zones, seek to remain comfortable without challenging themselves, and therefore do not achieve the success that is available. God wants us to have success because this is the process by which we grow and progress. Whereas the scriptures do not talk much about goal-setting techniques, they give many examples of overcoming personal fear, using courage to follow God's will, and learning to grow and progress.

ACTION EXERCISES

1. Write down ten goals that you want to achieve in the next twelve months.
2. Prioritize them from most important to least important.
3. Begin today working on the most important goal you have.
4. Make the goal specific, measurable, action-oriented, realistic, and timely.
5. Do the same for all ten goals.

Notes

1. Brian Tracy, *Million Dollar Habits* (Canada: Entrepreneur Press, 2004), 15.
2. *USA Today,* Feb. 2003. Quoted in Brian Tracy, *Million Dollar Habits*, 79.
3. Brian Tracy, *Eat That Frog* (San Francisco, CA: Berrett-Koehler Pub. Inc., 2001).
4. Marvin J. Ashton, "Progress through Change," *Ensign*, Nov. 1979, 61.
5. Hyrum Smith, *The Ten Natural Laws of successful Time and Life Management* (New York: Warner Books, 1994).
6. Howard W. Hunter, in Conference Report, April 1967, 117.
7. William H. Bennett, "Inertia," *Ensign*, May 1974, 33.

9 ACTION PLAN

For behold, if Adam had put forth his hand immediately, and partaken of the tree of life, he would have lived forever, according to the word of God, having no space for repentance; yea, and also the word of God would have been void, and the great plan of salvation would have been frustrated.

—ALMA 42:5

Setting good goals is a necessary first step, but without an action plan to establish those goals, no change will occur. This is the moment in which you decide how to put into practice the goals you have chosen. You need to break down long-term outcome goals into yearly goals, monthly schedules, and daily progress. If I want to improve my health as my outcome goal and I have decided that the first step is to lose sixty pounds this year, then I have to decide how I am going to do that. It would seem logical to just break that down into five pounds per month, which seems quite plausible. But how am I going to lose those five pounds per month? What changes am I going to make in my eating habits and in my activity level? I have tried to lose weight in the past and have never managed to keep the pounds off. What have I learned from past mistakes? What am I going to do differently? What obstacles will slow my progress or discourage me? How will I overcome them? These are some of the questions you need to ask before you formulate your plan.

The master planner of all is our Heavenly Father, and his plan is called the plan of salvation. He did not just dump us all on a planet and say, "Let's see what happens." He had a detailed plan. First he created us spiritually and kept us with him to learn, progress, and grow. He knew that this progress was limited, so he had to create a way for us to obtain our second estate and receive a physical body. This meant creating an earth that would sustain our physical bodies. It involved populating the earth with plants and animals to use for food, company, and work. It required providing us with light and darkness, mountains and fertile valleys. All the details of this earth were first programmed and planned long before they were actualized. In addition, God created family units with parents to support us physically, emotionally, and spiritually while we were young. Millions of details were worked out before the creation even began. God called this master plan, or blueprint, the spiritual creation. It was in place before the physical creation began. Part of the plan was to find a way that we could progress spiritually, become like our Father, and return to his presence. He knew that this meant putting us to the test, creating a veil that would cloud our memories of him and heaven, and sending a savior to pay for our sins and provide the way for us to repent. He didn't just make the plan and enforce it, but he involved all his children in the process. We voted to follow his plan; we chose to come to earth. Some of us were able to choose when we could come to earth and in which family we would belong. Many noble spirits helped God create the earth, and we cried hosanna in admiration of his plan.

Do you have a blueprint for your personal progress? Just as no engineer would build a house without first creating blueprints for all the details of the construction—the plumbing, the electric system, and so on—we, too, should create an action plan to achieve the goals that we have established. There are three steps to this plan.

First, break down your goal into manageable tasks. What are all the different behaviors you need in order to obtain your outcome goal? One way to identify manageable tasks was discussed in the introduction. Divide a sheet of paper into a chart that has three columns: "To Have," "To Do," and "To Be." The "To Have" column is your outcome goal. You may want to have better health, more peace and serenity in your relationship with your children, or a better income to provide for your family and others. The "To Do" column is the action plan. What are the steps necessary to achieve that goal? For health, it could be a variety of actions, including losing weight, exercising regularly, eating more fresh fruits and vitamins, not eating at fast food restaurants, taking medications, and having regular medical checkups. You have to identify all the tasks that make up your goal. For health, I usually list six or more tasks, but for success on the job, I might list more. To have peace in the home, you might decide that just two or three tasks are sufficient. The better you can analyze the problem and break it into separate tasks, the easier it is to make a plan.

Next, you must decide if these tasks are sequential or if you can work at them all at the same time. You may decide, for example, that you just want to focus on two for this year: exercising and eating fresh fruits. You may hope that by doing these things regularly you will still lose weight and you won't need to take vitamins. For success in business, you may wish to just concentrate on better time management this year and develop the habits that sustain this important goal. The process you are following is first defining all the tasks to do to achieve your goal, and then prioritizing them according to urgency or importance.

Elaine S. Dalton said,

> Your vision of your future will help you press forward. Take a few minutes to envision where you want to be in one year or two or five. Then take action to prepare yourselves. People do not just run a marathon when they decide to do it. They must train daily, slowly building stamina and endurance to run the 26.2-mile distance. So it is with life. It is daily diligence with prayer and scripture study that will help you reach your goals. Your daily decisions will influence generations.[1]

Nephi had the outcome goal of arriving in the promised land. Part of what he had to do was build a ship. He found, however, that before he could build the ship he needed tools, and to build the tools he had to find the ore to create iron. To do this he needed to build a smelter and bellows and the equipment to mine the ore. As a result, he had to define and prioritize them all the different tasks necessary to achieve his purpose. Then he had to go and do the work.

No engineer tries to keep his blueprints in his head. He writes out his plan, and details are added until the blueprint is complete. In the same way, it is not sufficient, if you truly desire success, to just think these things through. Write them down, create a plan, and write out the details. The next step is to create a schedule. Having a timetable creates urgency and challenges you to follow the plan. The Lord did not say he would create the earth when he felt like it. He had a plan and a timetable to complete it.

When someone starts a new business and goes to the bank for financing, the first thing the bank official wants to see is a business plan. He or she wants to see if you have worked out all the details of how you are going to run the business, including marketing, advertisement, daily functioning, cash flow, and so on. This is what we should do in each area of our endeavors. Obviously, I never had a detailed plan on how I was going to lose weight in all those years except to "diet." I had never analyzed what obstacles I would have to face, and neither did I work out strategies to overcome those difficulties. I never studied in my mind how I could keep myself motivated, nor did I think how to overcome my dislike for exercise, or what to do when I was depressed and wanted to eat sweets for emotional relief. My plan was "go on a diet!" It stayed the same for over twenty years, and I was always surprised that I did not get anywhere.

Most of us have spent our lives thinking that we should change things, but the reason we don't is that we aren't committed to a plan of action with a schedule to follow. We do not like to be pressured; we prefer to procrastinate. If this is how you feel about having goals and a plan, you need to return to step one. Is this something that you truly desire? Are you motivated by your own internal needs, or do you just feel that this is something you *should* do? Is it coming from within, or do you feel pressured by society, your family, your parents, or just your sense of responsibility? The secret to distinguishing outside pressures from internal desires is just this: if the whole idea of creating goals and an action plan creates stress and resistance, then you probably do not really desire these results. When, instead, the desire comes from within, then we are thankful for any tool or any suggestion that will help us achieve that goal more efficiently. The most heartbreaking event in life is to work for years toward goals that really are not what we desired. Parental expectations, social pressures, or a false sense of responsibility are not good reasons to try to achieve success. As Stephen Covey has said, too often we can work all our life to climb the ladder of success only to find that it is leaning on the wrong wall.[2]

If, instead, the problem is only our own laziness, then remember what the Lord has said about procrastination in Alma: "And now, as I said unto you before, as ye have had so many witnesses, therefore, I beseech of you that ye do not procrastinate the day of your repentance until the end; for after this day of life, which is given us to prepare for eternity, behold, if we do not improve our time while in this life, then cometh the night of darkness wherein there can be no labor performed" (Alma 34:33).

Ideally, our plan should let us know what we should be doing day by day to achieve our goal. We should be able to include in our daily plan some action or tasks that will bring us closer to our goal. We should remember that positive actions are always better than negative. Rather than deciding to not eat fatty foods, it is better to write down and think about the nutritious foods we want to eat. Remember, our mind concentrates on our dominant thoughts, and our unconscious mind is not receptive to negatives. For example, if I tell you not to think of a pink elephant with donkey ears, what immediately comes to mind? When you think, "I cannot eat sweets today," you are actually focusing your mind on sweets, increasing your attention on anything sweet and increasing your desire for sugar. Think positive. Think about how good an apple tastes and how much you desire to eat one, and it will become your dominant thought. This is true for any bad habit. If you have a problem with swearing, you cannot think, "I won't say ____." You must come up with alternative words or phrases that are positive to say and then practice them so that they will become your automatic and dominant response. I learned this principle in the garden. If you weed your garden and leave nicely overturned earth but don't plant any flowers or shrubs, your nice free patch will soon turn to weeds again. If you only work on eliminating the negatives of your life, whether it be eating sweets or getting rid of debts, but never learn to plant the positives, your plan will not work. You must learn to love fresh fruits and vegetables or at least some good foods and include them in your diet, or once your resistance to sweets diminishes you will be right back where you started. In the same way, you must learn the techniques of saving and learn to love having money in the bank or you will always be in debt.

You will notice that one of your columns is still empty. What is the "To Be" column? This is where many of our best plans fail. This column deals with whether or not we are the type of person who can carry out the "To Do" action plan. If I have made a wonderful action plan in which I will exercise forty-five minutes every day but am not a self-disciplined person who regularly carries out any type of program every day, what will happen to my wonderful plan? If I am not a disciplined person who is able to create a routine, I either have to come up with some other strategy, or I have to make it a priority to develop self-discipline. Before Nephi could build the ship, or even the tools, he needed to find and mine the ore. But what if he were not a practical-minded person and didn't like to do physical labor? Would he have ever accomplished what he did? What would he need to develop first?

We have to first focus on the "To Be" list and see if it corresponds to the list that we have made from a previous chapter regarding our strengths and weaknesses. Make out your "To Be" list and compare it to the list you made previously. Are you trying to achieve your goals through your strengths or your weaknesses? If it is your weaknesses, then you are fighting a losing battle. It is our strengths that will help us achieve success, not our weaknesses. Identifying one of your weaknesses and making a goal to improve is good, but the goals that lead to your success must be based on your strengths. If you are a creative person and get bored easily with routine things, doing the same exercise routine at the same time every day probably won't work for you. You need to liven it up with a variety of different exercises. You can swim one day, do aerobics another, and use your love for gardening to supplement the other days. Use your passions and your strong points to achieve your goals, and you will see dramatic improvement. At least 80 percent of what is on the "to be" list in your action plan should be taken from your strengths and passions. If you absolutely need to develop an attribute to achieve what you want in life, this must become your priority goal, and other objectives will have to be put on the back burner.

Once you have made a list of the tasks that you must perform to achieve your objective and you have created a schedule with deadlines for when each task must be performed, you are now able to evaluate your progress. This means that before you begin any action at all, you need to know exactly where you are. For example, if you want to be healthier and lose weight, you need to accurately list how you eat right now. Before you change anything, make a daily log of what you eat, how much you eat, and why you eat what you do. Are you eating from boredom, to offset depression or anxiety, and so on? Weigh yourself every day to create a baseline, and measure the circumference of your waist, chest, thighs, and arms. Write it all down and keep it as your standard of comparison.

Next, write down an analysis of all the problems you believe you will encounter. This can be based on what has happened in the past. If your goal is to reduce the fighting between your children and increase the good and pleasant communication, after you have accurately measured how often the fighting takes place, how many kind words you say to them and they say to each other, at what time it occurs each day and some of the reasons, then sit down and list all the obstacles that you envision you will face when you enact change. Making an accurate log of the behaviors allows you to see some of the causes of what is happening, and this can become part of your plan. For example, if you notice that fighting occurs in mid-afternoon, then maybe a nutritious snack will help, and this would become part of the action plan. Look at what you have done in the past and examine why it has not worked and search for different ways to change. This is where preparation comes into play. We need new information and new perception to allow change. Create strategies for how you are going to handle the fighting differently. Do not try to do everything at once. Practice one or two strategies for a month or two until they become habits. Remember to keep accurate measurements.

Each day, each week, each month you need to determine the progress you have made. At the end of each day, you should take out your action plan, look at what you have done, and write a "to do" list for the following day. You should analyze what you have done right and what still needs progress. If your strategy is not working, you need to evaluate why and either change the strategy or go back and see if there are other skills you need to develop first. You should be working toward at least one of your long-term goals every day. If days pass and you are making no progress, then something is wrong and you may need to reevaluate. Possibly other things have gotten in the way and have become urgent. Hyrum Smith Jr. said, "You should never let things that are urgent get in the way of things that are important."[3] Remember that achieving this success is your highest priority. Reschedule your priorities and make time for your goal. If the problem persists, perform a deeper analysis of what is wrong. You may want to ask yourself:

- What problem is impeding my progress?
- Do I still ardently desire this goal?
- Were my expectations realistic?
- What can I learn from this setback to better attack the problem?
- Is there a better way to reach my goal?
- Do I need outside help to reach my objective?
- Do I need to develop other qualities first?

If you do not constantly evaluate your progress, days will slip by, weeks will pass, and before you know it a year will have passed and you will have made no progress. This just adds to your discouragement. If your plan is not working, you have to find out why and modify the plan. One of the first places to look is your "To Be" list. Is there a weakness that does not allow progress? Can you find another strategy to overcome the weakness with one of your strengths?

Perotta's law, a rule used in management, states that 20 percent of your effort creates 80 percent of your results. Learn what the 20 percent is for you and your goals, and concentrate on that. For example, if you want to be more successful on the job, you must identify the most important aspects of the job that will give you the highest return on your efforts. What are the tasks that make up the 20 percent of your job that generates 80 percent of the results you are seeking? Any improvement has to focus in this area of your job performance. Changing behaviors that have little impact on your overall performance will make no difference to your career.[4]

Therefore, an action plan takes your goals and breaks them down into manageable bits that you can improve day by day. It provides an analysis of what you need to do and the difficulties you will probably encounter. It includes different strategies to achieve those tasks and provides a daily and weekly evaluation of your progress. Start each day with a clear idea of what you need to accomplish that day to move toward your goal. End the day with an evaluation of what you have achieved. Make this part of your daily prayers and ask the Lord for his help in all you do.

ACTION EXERCISES

1. Study the list of your outcome goals and performance goals and decide which goal is your top priority. Decide which of these goals you are most committed to achieving.
2. Make a baseline measurement of how you are performing in that area right now before you have attempted any change. Keep a daily log, and list all the behaviors that affect that goal.
3. Analyze your log, and analyze your past attempts to change that behavior. Decide on one or two strategies for change that you need to enact right now. Decide how you will overcome the problems that arise, and include that in your strategy.
4. Break down the change you want to make into daily behaviors that you can measure.
5. Decide who you need to help you make these changes, and ask their participation, advice, and support.
6. Begin by changing one or two behaviors at a time, and work on these daily until they become a habit.

7. Evaluate your progress daily with a partner. Focus immediately on the difficulties you are having, and evolve new strategies to overcome them.
8. Pray daily for the Lord's help in achieving this change.

Notes

1. Elaine S. Dalton, "Press Forward and Be Steadfast," *Ensign*, May 2003, 105.
2. Stephen R. Covey, *The Seven Habits of Highly Effective People* (New York: Simon & Schuster, 1989).
3. Hyrum Smith, *The Ten Natural Laws of Successful Time and Life Management* (New York: Warner Books, 1994).
4. Brian Tracy, *Change Your Thinking Change Your Life* (New Jersey: John Wiley & Sons, Inc., 2003), 112.

STEP 3

TAKE ACTION

So far, you have dedicated your time and effort to preparing yourself. The better your preparation is, the more success you will have. There comes a time, however, when we must decide that we have prepared as well as we can and we must now act.

We must implement our action plan. The first step is to involve others in what we are doing. This increases our commitment and provides support for our goals. We must overcome our pride and ask others for help, particularly those closest to us.

Then, we must develop the habits necessary for our success. There are many habits that characterize successful people; the more successful habits that we acquire, the faster we can move toward our goal. Finally, we achieve all goals only through hard work and diligence. We must take responsibility for our behavior and act with diligence.

THE STEPS TO SUCCESS

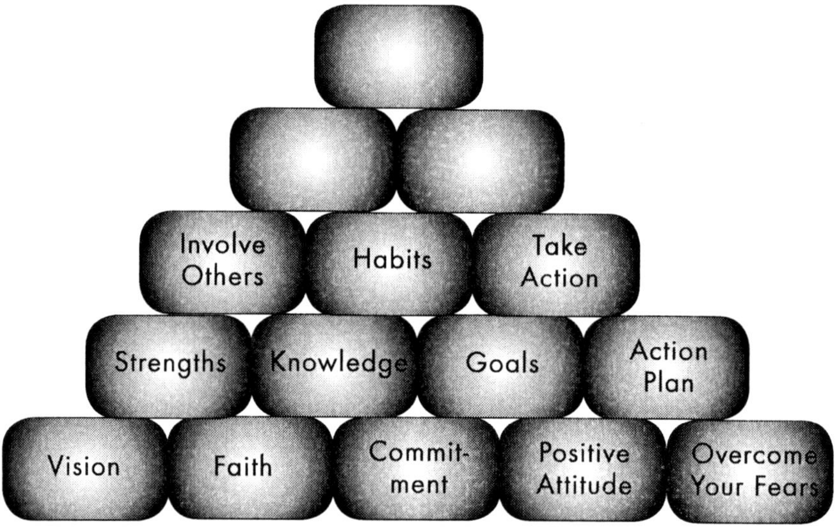

10 INVOLVE OTHERS

We without them cannot be made perfect; neither can they without us be made perfect.
—D&C 128:18

You cannot do it alone. No one has ever achieved success by himself. We need the help of other people to achieve our goals. Our success will be directly proportional to how we are able to work with our friends, family, coworkers, and the Lord.

The first person's support we need in our project is the Lord. Without his help we are handicapped. Philippians 4:13, which states, "I can do all things through Christ which strengtheneth me," is one of the most powerful scriptures we have. If we observe the prophets, what strikes us most is that whatever their endeavor, whether temporal or spiritual, they seek the help and counsel of the Lord. The method to obtain the Lord's help is through prayer, and when we need a great deal of help, we need to both fast and pray. Look at Ammon and his brothers: "They waxed strong in the knowledge of the truth; for they were men of sound understanding and they had searched the scriptures diligently, that they might know the word of God. But this is not all; they had given themselves to much prayer and fasting; therefore they had the spirit of prophecy, and the spirit of revelation, and when they taught, they taught with power and authority of God" (Alma 17:2–3).

Alma 34 teaches us to pray to the Lord in all our doings: "Yea, humble yourselves, and continue in prayer unto him. Cry unto him when ye are in your fields, yea, over all your flocks. Yea, and when you do not cry unto the lord, let your hearts be full, drawn out in prayer unto him continually for your welfare, and also for the welfare of those who are around you" (Alma 34:19–20, 27).

I have placed involving others at this point of the book because it is easier to have others' support once we have an action plan and know exactly what help we need. However, the earlier we involve the Lord and those close to us, the more success we will have at each step of our progress. We can only have faith in our project if we know that it meets the approval of the Lord. Prayer is not a one-time event but a constant communion with the Lord to ask his assistance each day to achieve our goals and overcome all difficulties. The scriptures use the term "fervent prayer," which is a deep conviction from our heart, not just words repeated without thought.

After the Lord, we need our spouse. The Lord said, "It is not good that man be alone; wherefore, I will make a help meet for him" (Moses 3:18). You and your spouse are a team and need each other's approval, emotional support, and active participation in order to achieve any type of success. Those who desire success in their career may need to work extra hours, take business trips, and dedicate much time and energy to work. Trying to do this without the support of their spouses will only lead to conflict. Both have to agree that this success is for the benefit of the family. It has to be a joint decision and a joint sacrifice. Then and only then will they be free to commit to their goal.

I learned this at my own expense. I began writing a book, became discouraged, left the project, and was sidetracked by other events. Then, I started feeling strongly that I should dedicate myself to writing. I decided to take a six-month break from teaching at the university and dedicate myself to finishing the book. I discussed this with my wife, Fernanda, but I did not really express how deeply I felt about this, nor the fact that I had planned alternative work to allow me to both work and write. I took it for granted that she would support me. Instead, she only saw that I was leaving my regular job for a fancy that did not have any security. This made her highly anxious; she started working extra hours to earn more and resented what I was doing. This led to further misunderstandings between us, to the point that it started ruining our relationship. Needless to say, I did not finish the book, and it was not until several years later that I was able to involve her in my desire to write and gain her support. The irony of this was that I was writing a book on marriage relations! I learned that if you are a team, there is no place for individualism disregarding the other team members.

If you aren't married, you are missing an important person for your personal achievement, but there are others you can involve. Seek the support of friends, other family members, support groups, coworkers, or a mentor. The more people you can involve as part of your plan, the better and faster you can achieve success. Some authors suggest that we create our own personal dream team, that is, a group of people who each contributes their knowledge or skills to help us achieve our goals.

On the job, the easiest way to gain the skills and knowledge we need is to find someone who has those skills and enlist their help. Seeking out a mentor is considered the most secure way to having success on the job. If you are a salesman, go to the best salesperson in your company and ask him how he is able to achieve so much. Observe what he does, follow his example. In any job, there is always someone who is the best; seek him or her out and ask for help. Go to your supervisor and ask him or her what skills you need to develop in order to have more success on the job. Enroll in courses or seminars that will better prepare you for your job. Use your mentor's knowledge and assistance to grow.

Often we are embarrassed to ask for help. We think that we should do projects on our own. Unfortunately, this attitude is quite diffused and limits the progress of many people. How much progress you make in any endeavor depends very much on how well you work with other people.

Most people find it easier and more enjoyable to exercise with someone else. Having someone who will walk with you, jog with you, or do any other exercise plan increases your commitment. You know that they will be there, so you are forced to get up and jog even on those days that you have no desire. You can motivate each other, talk together, and make your exercise routines more interesting.

Losing weight requires a support group. You will most likely need to completely change eating habits, which will involve the whole family. You need the support and understanding of your family members. Often you will be changing their eating habits too, and if they are not equally committed, they will sabotage your efforts. Get a support group; join Weight Watchers or some other group-dieting plan. Changing long established habits takes incredible effort in the beginning to overcome the inertia of years of poor lifestyle. The more difficult the goal, the more support you need from the people around you.

When one parent decides to change their parenting style, they need the understanding, support, and commitment of the other parent. Your spouse may continue their style, but they shouldn't sabotage what you are trying to do. Better yet, try to actively involve them in your action plan. If they are not willing, or you are a single parent, enlist the help of a neighbor, a relative, or a friend. You need someone you can go to with your frustrations and who can provide another prospective.

Those who live alone can still find people who can help. The Internet is the biggest network of people that has ever existed. No matter what your interest or problem is, there are people out there who share it. Contact them. Get involved in their discussion, enlist their help, and offer your advice. Join a forum or chat group of single parents, frustrated mothers, or whatever will help you gain more insight into what you want to achieve. There are literally thousands of personal coaches online who specialize in a variety of areas from relationships to financial success to personal growth counsel. You should be selective in who you choose since not all are equally qualified, but often they can offer a different perspective or solution to your problems.

Your dream team of people to assist you in your quest for excellence need not come from only the people you know or people living today. You have the knowledge and advice of centuries of special people you can go to. Find the people you admire the most and read their biographies and their own works so that in any situation you can ask, how would they solve this problem? Read about Jack Welch or Bill Gates and how they achieved their business success, and use that as part of your action plan. Use the scriptures and the prophets. If you are working on becoming a better parent, find all the scriptures that deal with parenting and read them constantly. Find all the examples of good parenting and bad parenting from the scriptures and meditate on them. Let Alma be your role model as he intensely and repeatedly prays for his son. Read about the modern prophets and read their words in the *Ensign* and other Church publications. Let these men of God be part of your dream team for success. Each time you need encouragement, you can go to one of them in your mind and ask, "Abraham, what do you have to say to me today? How would you solve this problem?" The more intimately you get to know these role models, the better they can help you.

Unfortunately, in America we have the myth of the lone ranger, the hero who goes out and solves the world's problems all alone. We are an individualistic society, and we often believe that everyone should be able to solve his own difficulties. This is not the Lord's formula at all. Repeatedly the Lord commands us to love one another. "A new commandment I give unto you, That ye love one another; as I have loved you, that ye also love one another. By this shall all men know that ye are my disciples, if ye love one another" (John 13:34–35). Is not love being there for one another, helping each other overcome difficulties and supporting each other? One of the last instructions Jesus gave to his disciples was "and when thou art converted, strengthen thy brethren" (Luke 22:32).

Whether we are working to obtain our salvation or to achieve earthly goals, the Lord expects us to work together. The principle of unity is eternal and necessary for our salvation. The Lord asks us to be one. He does not tell us to be alone nor to ask for help to become isolated. That is the doctrine of Satan. The gospel of Christ is a gospel of love and unity, with each person helping those near him so we can all progress and achieve our goals.

John Wooden said, "It is amazing how much can be accomplished when no one cares who gets the credit."[1] This also implies that not only do we need the help of others, but that our success in life and most of our goals depend on our becoming involved in the lives of others. Brian Tracy calls this the law of giving and states, "The law of giving says the more you give of yourself without expectation of return, the more that will come back to you from the most unexpected sources."[2]

You cannot remain isolated and be successful. You must become a people person. You need to be receptive to the needs of other people. Learn to recognize the needs of the people near you at home, on the job, and in your everyday life. Often it takes very little to be personable and likable. Abraham Lincoln once said, "Everybody likes a compliment."[3] Smile; give compliments; remember people's names and something about them. These small things make all the difference in relationships. Be proactive in giving of your time and talents. This is not a calculated means to success but a sincere interest in others and in helping to lighten their load. Alma asked those who wanted to be baptized, "And now, as ye are desirous to come into the fold of God, and to be called his people, and are willing bear one another's burdens, that they be light; Yea and are willing to mourn with those who mourn; yea, and comfort those that stand in need of comfort. . . . Now I say unto you, if this be the desire of your hearts, what have you against being baptized in the name of the Lord?" (Mosiah 18:8–10). This is part of the covenant in becoming God's people.

> In putting people first, the "Open Sesame" of human relationships is to "make others feel important." Making others feel important satisfies the deepest subconscious craving of human nature. Everything you do or fail to do can be judged against this standard. Does it make people feel more important or less important? That is the question."[4]
>
> —BRIAN TRACY

Another way to work well with other people and to make them feel appreciated and valued is to listen attentively to what they have to say. This is probably the most important key to good relationships in the home, and it is equally effective on the job or in church. Do you listen attentively to what your children say and acknowledge their input? Do you listen to your spouse—not just hearing their words but empathizing with their emotions and sharing their thoughts and feelings? If you practice this in the home and use it in all walks of life, you will find that you will draw people to you and at the same time learn from others.

Several authors state that the key to success in any field is to volunteer. Every organization needs help. Join an organization in the field that you are interested in and volunteer to help. You will soon find yourself immersed in work, but you will also be making friends and contacts that may become invaluable. The old adage that it is not what you know but who you know that makes the difference is true. People hire, help, or support the people they already know, admire, and trust. The Lord calls this service and says, "And behold, I tell you these things that ye may learn wisdom; that ye may learn that when ye are in the service of your fellow beings ye are only in the service of your God" (Mosiah 2:17). Consciously and deliberately seek opportunities to serve. If you are trying to be a better parent, participate in those activities involving your children, whether it be with the school, sport groups, church activities, or any other. You will become more involved in the life of your children, better understand their needs, and positively influence the groups that affect their lives.

> Treasure the love you receive above all. It will survive long after your gold and good health have vanished.[5]
>
> —OG MANDINO

You will not arrive at success alone. We need the help of other people and they need ours. Make this part of your formula for success and you will be surprised at the results.

ACTION EXERCISES

1. Look at your action plan and evaluate how much you have involved others in your plan. If you are trying to do it alone, you need to make a change.
2. Pray mightily to the Lord for your success.
3. Write down how you can involve your spouse and family members in your plan. Evaluate what special talents they have that could help you. Show them your plan and ask for their suggestions. Be humble enough to recognize that they may have ideas that are better than yours.
4. Examine your circle of friends, your coworkers, and your supervisor. Identify their talents and decide the skills they have that you can use to achieve your goals.
5. Find a mentor at work. Go to him or her, and ask for help and advice.
6. Read biographies of people you admire. Find books written by people in your field. Pick your personal dream team of advisors. Go back often and read their works.
7. Selectively find all the scriptures that can help you overcome your difficulties or inspire you to achieve your results. Review these scriptures daily. Find in the scriptures prophets or people who have solved your same problems. Meditate on how they have done it and how you can apply it to your life.
8. Look for organizations you could join to meet new people, or find out how you could participate more fully in those organizations to which you already belong. Volunteer your talents. Find ways to serve.
9. Make becoming a people person part of your "to be" list. Compliment your spouse often. Focus on remembering people's names. Smile often. Move outside your narrow world and see how you can lighten the load of others around you.
10. Develop the habit of listening attentively to others. Stop yourself from jumping in and making your comments, and just listen.

Pay close attention to the verbal and nonverbal messages that are sent and give feedback.

11. Develop the habit of praising your family members and people around you. Compliment often. Use one-minute praise sessions with family, coworkers, and employees.

Notes

1. Brian D. Biro, *Beyond Success* (Hamilton, Montana: Pygmalion Press, 1995), 235.
2. Brian Tracy, *Create Your Own Future* (Hobeken, NJ: John Wiley & Sons, 2002), 119.
3. Ibid.
4. Brian Tracy, *Million Dollar Habits* (Canada: Entrepreneur Press, 2004), 176.
5. Available from www.thinkexist.com.

11 HABITS

Therefore, I beseech of you that you do not procrastinate the day of your repentance until the end; for after this day of life, which is given us to prepare for eternity, behold, if we do not improve our time while in this life, then cometh the night of darkness wherein there can be no labor performed.

—ALMA 34:33

In psychology, it is said that our brain is a "cognitive miser." Our brain is constructed to think as little as possible. Most of us are on auto-pilot most of the day. We have our routines and patterns that take us through the day, and if something new or unexpected happens, we have to turn on our brains and think of a solution or process new information. We create mental templates or "schemas" to deal with most of what we do or think based on past experiences. This series of schemas then creates our comfort zone. As long as we are following old patterns we are comfortable and do not need to activate our plan. No anxiety is generated, no fear is triggered, and everything just stays the same. The problem, of course, is that as long as we stay in our comfort zone, we are not growing. As long as we follow our old habits we will not change. Five years from now you will be the same person you are today unless you change what you are doing.

We are creatures of habit. Experts estimate that 95 percent of what we do and think is the result of habit.[1] If we normally operate on habit, then we will do good things without much effort if we have developed good habits. If we do not have many good habits, the sooner we can establish them, the easier the rest of our lives will be. It is an investment of time and energy that pays off over the years. Changing a habit or creating a new habit, however, requires intense mental activity over a long period of time, and your brain will resist it.

It has been said that creating a habit requires consciously, deliberately repeating the same activity over and over every day for at least twenty-one consecutive days. If you miss a day, you must begin again. This is not always the case, as some habits are easier to create than others and some behaviors are harder to change than others. But doing something over and over for twenty-one days is a good beginning.

> The individual who wants to reach the top in business must appreciate the might of the force of habit—and must understand that practices are what create habits. He must be quick to break those habits that can break him—and hasten to adopt those practices that will become the habits that help him achieve the success he desires.[2]
>
> —JOHN PAUL GETTY

Many researchers have examined the differences between successful people (in any field) and average or unsuccessful people. All studies have shown that successful people have created good habits that reinforce, or sometimes create, their success. The following are eight habits that characterize successful people:

1. Successful people get up early.

Benjamin Franklin said centuries ago, "Early to bed, early to rise makes a man healthy, wealthy and wise." The Lord has stated in D&C 88: "Cease to sleep longer than is needful; retire to bed early, that ye be not weary; arise early, that your bodies and your mind may be invigorated" (v. 124). Can you imagine a successful CEO, entrepreneur, spiritual leader, or teacher hitting the snooze button repeatedly, getting up late, hurrying to get ready, rushing through traffic, cursing all the slow drivers, and arriving late at work every day? It just does not happen. Getting up early is almost a universal principle for success. This is when successful people plan their day and when they meditate and collect themselves for all they have to do. Often this is the time that they dedicate to exercise. Not only do they get up early, often at five or six o'clock, but they use this time in the morning for their personal benefit. All successful businessmen arrive early to work. They often accomplish more in the hour before the other workers arrive than many people achieve by noon.

If you want to have success in any area of life, begin the day early and use it for yourself. Meditate on what you want to accomplish. Use it to exercise, read the scriptures, and pray, and you will be surprised how your day changes. How many of us do not find the time for ourselves to read, study, meditate, and pray? How often have you said, "I would like to keep a journal, but I just do not have the time"? The time is there. Use it.

2. Successful people use time wisely.

The one thing that most separates the successful person from the failure and the rich from the poor is how they use their free time. Time is the most precious element we have, and successful people use it wisely. Each day they review their long-term and short-term goals and make "to do" lists of what they have to accomplish. Most important, they prioritize their list to distinguish between important and less important tasks, and they work on the important tasks first. One way of prioritizing is to use the ABCDE method. Next to each task, write A if it is both important to your goals and urgent—it must be accomplished today. You should not have more than three or four "A" items and you can further prioritize them as A-1, A-2, and so on. "B" tasks are those that would be good to accomplish today, but they are either less important or less urgent. "C" tasks are those that are not particularly important. "D" tasks are those that you can delegate to someone else, and "E" tasks are those that might have been urgent or important at one time but no longer are; you can eliminate these. Begin working on task A-1, and continue until you have accomplished your most important task; then begin on A-2. You should always be working on the most important tasks that you have to do during the day. Never spend time with C tasks just because they are easier when you still have A and B tasks to accomplish. The same is true for B tasks when there are more important things to do. If you are always working on what is most important, you will accomplish twice as much or more than your coworkers.[3]

All successful people know and follow Perotta's law. Twenty percent of your work produces 80 percent of your results. The wisdom of success is to determine the 20 percent of effort that produces the 80 percent of your results. This is true in whatever field you are trying to obtain success. Decide what the 20 percent of effort in your relationship with your spouse or children is that will reap the greatest results in harmony and love. Who are the 20 percent of clients that will produce 80 percent of your income? What is the one thing that if you changed it today would most increase your health, wealth, or spirituality? Determine what that is and then begin focusing you efforts on that.

3. Successful people keep their energy levels high.

If time is our most precious commodity, then health and energy to use that time comes immediately after, and successful people know that. When you want to have success and you want to accomplish all you can, you must make health a priority. This means getting your weight under control, eating nutritiously, and exercising regularly. Some of the guidelines that successful people follow are to eat fresh fruits and vegetables regularly. Unfortunately, our society emphasizes processed foods, which usually have high quantities of salt and sugar and few vitamins or minerals. Drink water and large quantities of water daily. Avoid soda high in caffeine and sugar; avoid diet sodas that stimulate hunger. Drink water instead. Experts recommend that an average adult should drink at least eight, eight-ounce glasses of water daily. Avoid fast food restaurants with food that has high quantities of fats, salts, and sugars and little nutrition. Eat smaller meals and light snacks several times a day. Avoid big starchy meals that take away energy from your mind for digestion.

Exercise regularly. Walk, jog, swim, use a bicycle, garden, use the stairs, go to aerobic classes, or work out with weights. Become active in any way possible. Exercise at least thirty minutes, at least three or four times weekly. Make it a habit. Successful people do.

If you get up early, you must go to bed early. You need your rest. The average person needs seven to eight hours of sleep a night to rest properly. You cannot have sufficient energy to accomplish all you need to do if you do not get enough rest. Americans in general do not sleep enough, and this leads to fatigue, stress, and depression—certainly not energized feelings. The other aspect of energy is a positive attitude, which is the next habit.

If you can complete mastery over self, you will easily master all else. To triumph over self is the perfect victory.[4]

—THOMAS A'KEMPIS

---

4. Successful people have positive attitudes.

Successful people cultivate a positive attitude. They are careful to have positive thoughts, positive self-talk, and a positive attitude toward others. You can do the same. The next time someone asks how you are, answer "great" or "fantastic." Can you imagine Jesus going around with slumped shoulders saying things like, "I'm hanging in there" or "All right I guess"? Monitor your thoughts, and make sure they are positive. If you find yourself in the dumps, stop yourself and change. Attitude is a choice. You can often change your emotions by acting as if you feel good, and within a short time you will lift your feelings and will feel more positive.

You are responsible for your emotions. If you let others or outside consequences determine how you feel, you put the control of your life in their hands. Remember that what you say to yourself is the key to how you feel. If it is raining outside, saying "Oh, what a lousy day" will make you feel miserable for the rest of the day. Find something positive. Say to yourself, "Rain is so refreshing," or thank the Lord for the rain. Then you will feel better. Do not let the weather, your coworkers, the other drivers on the road, or anyone else determine your attitude.

Nothing depletes energy more than a depressed attitude. You can eat energizing food and exercise regularly, but if you are depressed, you only mope around. You are miserable and you depress the people around you. If the depression is too deep and you need help, get medication or seek counseling. Otherwise, avoid depressing thoughts, work on your attitude, examine your self-esteem, and start sending positive messages to yourself.

5. Successful people are concerned for others and make them feel important.

If your success depends on *who* you know and not *what* you know, it stands to reason that developing good people skills is vital to success. The secret to having good people skills is to make everyone you meet feel important. The first and most important ingredient costs nothing; all you need to do is smile. Everyone is attracted to a person who smiles. A smile is an indication of a positive, joyful attitude, and people like to be with positive people.

A second secret that most successful people have mastered is to remember people's names and something about them. Our memory stores what is important to us, and when you cannot remember someone's name, it is an indication to them that you do not care enough about them to remember. If you have a problem remembering names, read books or take courses dedicated to different techniques of memory improvement.

A third secret is the attitude of humility. Do you believe that you can learn something from everyone? Successful people show interest in other people and their ideas. They have mastered the art of asking people questions about their life, their job, and their family, and then they listen with attention. Good listening is an art that serves in all walks of life.

> The beginning of a habit is like an invisible thread, but every time we repeat the act, we strengthen the strand, add to it another filament, until it becomes a great cable and binds us irrevocably in thought and act.[5]
>
> —ORISON SWETT MARDEN

---

6. Successful people constantly expand their comfort zones.

Successful people are always searching for new ideas because they know that any idea may be the solution to a problem (or a potential problem) or may be a new opportunity to earn more. Leaders constantly seek ways to expand their talents. They volunteer to manage projects, to give speeches, to participate in committees. They take on tasks that they have never tried before. They get involved in community service and church service. They do not reluctantly accept a calling in the Church but actively seek out ways to serve. Begin today by committing yourself to accept every opportunity to learn, expand your talents, and use them to serve others. Practice doing something new every day. Listen to different music, drive a different route home, read a new genre of magazine or book, find someone outside your usual circle of friends. Change the way you do things. Leave your comfort zone.

7. Successful people have balance in their lives.

A common fallacy of many people is thinking they need to operate in only one or two areas of their life. They spend most of their time working and the rest of their time at home. These are certainly important aspects, but we should realize that there are other aspects of life we should expand. Social relations, personal progress, physical improvement, intellectual challenges, and spirituality are all important. Experts on stress have found that the more we can balance all the different aspects of our lives, the better we feel and the more we control stress.

Good leaders know that work is not everything. They know that it is necessary to take time to meditate and pray, to spend times with friends and associates, and develop these relationships. They know that their family relationships are vital to their well-being. In an interesting study performed at Harvard,[6] 1,500 people selected from Who's Who in America were interviewed. The group included Nobel prize winners, industry leaders, politicians, scientists, and other leaders. When they were asked what were the most important results of their success, the top three answers were (1) respect of their parents (86 percent of the respondents mentioned this); (2) respect of their family and children; and (3) respect of their peers and colleagues.

8. Successful people have a grateful heart.

People who have accomplished much almost invariably recognize that it is not by just their efforts but through the help of the Lord or something superior to themselves. These are people who show humility and gratitude for what they have. Most leaders believe that they have been blessed in their life and that it is their duty to give back to the world. Most successful people give generously to charities, not just of their money but also of their time. Most believe that what they do with their talents and abilities should be dedicated not just to themselves but for the good of their company, society, and humanity. Paying your tithing willingly, being generous with your offerings, and working in your church callings to help others are all ways to show gratitude to the Lord. Counting your blessings daily and thanking the Lord in your prayers is another. Many leaders keep a gratitude journal in which they regularly write down all the things for which they can thank God. Few tools are so effective in creating a positive attitude. You cannot be thankful and negative at the same time. Every time you start feeling depressed, you can refer to your journal and it can lift your mood. Express gratitude not just to the Lord but to your spouse, your parents, your children, your friends, and your coworkers. Make gratitude an active part of your life and you will find yourself more positive and optimistic, and success will come to you.

Develop these habits that define successful people, and you cannot help but create success for yourself in whatever field you desire it.

Note

1. Brian Tracy, *Million Dollar Habits,* (Canada: Entrepreneur Press, 2004), 79.
2. Ibid.
3. Brian Tracy, *Focal Point* (New York: AMACOM, 2002).
4. Available from www.saidwhat.co.uk.
5. Orison Swett Marden, *Peace, Power & Plenty,* Cosimo Classics, Personal Development.
6. Brian Tracy, *Create Your Own Future* (Hobeken, NJ: John Wiley & Sons, 2002), 219.

12 TAKE ACTION

Wherefore, now let every man learn his duty, and to act in the office in which he is appointed, in all diligence. He that is slothful shall not be counted worthy to stand, and he that learns not his duty and shows himself not approved shall not be counted worthy to stand. Even so. Amen.

— D&C 107:99–100

Taking action is where most people fail. Either they jump in and act without proper preparation and a well-developed plan, or they procrastinate and hesitate and never get started. Many people spend years preparing to fulfill their dreams but never seem to arrive at a point where they take action. This is equally devastating. To succeed you must take purposeful action according to the plan you have created. Once you have set your goals and made a plan, you must focus your energy on your objectives. This is the moment in which your faith and commitment galvanize to make you act. Now, your positive thoughts and positive attitude keep you on your course as you direct your efforts with integrity to achieve your goal.

There are four aspects to action that you should consider: focus, overcoming procrastination, taking responsibility, and diligence.

1. Focus

Sunlight alone, however hot, does not provoke a fire. As everyone knows, however, if I channel the energy of the sunlight through a lens that converges the rays to one point, it is very easy to start a fire. The same is true for our energy. Your action plan must focus your energy toward your goals so that you can burn through all obstacles and succeed. Since it takes time to achieve these goals, many people lose their focus over time and fall back into old patterns and habits. You must keep your focus alive.

> I could never have done what I have done without the habits of punctuality, order and diligence, without the determination to concentrate myself on one subject at a time.[1]
>
> —CHARLES DICKENS

One of the ways to increase your focus is to constantly visualize your goal. Athletes discovered visualization in the sixties as sport psychology emerged for the first time. They found that creating the mental image of each step of their athletic performance in a relaxed state improved their game. The Russians experimented with this concept scientifically, having athletes spend different quantities of their time on visualization and actual training. They found that the more intricate the movements were, the more they benefited from visualization. For example, the pole vault is more complex than running the 800-meter dash, and figure skating is more intricate than speed racing. Therefore, these sports benefited more from visualization. The Russians found, however, that visualization benefited all physical activities, so most of their athletes spent at least 50 percent of their time in visualization and 50 percent in practice, and in some cases athletes were spending as much as 90 percent of their training in visualization. As a result, all great athletes today, from Tiger Woods to Lance Armstrong, use visualization regularly in their game.

Further studies have shown that when you visualize, you stimulate the same neural pathways as when you actually do the activity. Research in the seventies and eighties began to show that visualization is useful not just for physical activities but also for any objective we want to reach. The more we can visualize ourselves reaching our objective, the more we increase our commitment and we send messages to our own unconscious mind that this is what we are achieving. If you spend just five or ten minutes a day visualizing your goal, you activate all the motivational aspects of your brain to obtain that goal. You focus your energy for that day on what you are going to do and achieve and how you are going to accomplish it. Use visualization to focus both on your long-term outcome goals and your specific actions of the day.

For example, meditate and focus your mind to visualize first on your goal of having peace in your family. See yourself serene with your children, and see your serenity calm their frustrations and bickering. Keep this image in your mind. Then run through the specific strategy that you have created in your action plan for how you will deal with your children when they start to yell and fight. Visualize yourself in as much detail as possible dealing with the situation with a calm voice and with patience. See yourself gently redirecting your children to another activity while you ignore their screams, and see them quiet down and smile as you hold them. Go through these details while you are in a calm, relaxed state. Do it at once each morning, or more often, and you will see the effect on your actions. Visualization is the perfect practice of the mind to achieve our results and can be used for any situation.

If you are on a diet, first visualize yourself as you want to be. See yourself as a slender, healthy person full of energy, and couple this with positive affirmations that you repeat over and over. *I am slender and healthy. I feel great.* Visualize yourself in a wonderful outfit that enhances your new figure and visualize how great you feel. Run through the positive emotions in your mind, and you will motivate those same emotions. Now, visualize your strategy for the day. See yourself going to the fridge and taking out an apple. Feel the rich, tart flavor of the apple in your mouth and feel the satisfaction that you will achieve. See yourself eating a small portion of food and feeling invigorated and full of energy.

Visualization can be used to rehearse any future action. Use it to review and change in your mind anything that went wrong in the past and revise the events to create a positive result. Maybe you made a sales call that went all wrong. Visualize it in your mind and run it through several times, thinking of different solutions you could have experimented with. Then visualize it going perfectly with you saying exactly the right words and the client happy and smiling. Visualize the client signing the largest order you have ever received.

All people who have tried it find visualization one of the most effective tools in their lives. You can use it for virtually anything. Long before scientists discovered the power of visualization, the Lord first created things spiritually: "For I, the Lord God, created all things of which I have spoken, spiritually, before they were naturally on the face of the earth" (Moses 3:5). The Lord used first a mental plan and then a material plan to accomplish his goals.

Try it. Put it into practice every day. Take ten minutes that you have created for yourself in the morning by getting up earlier and visualize all the positive actions that you want to accomplish. Then end the session with a prayer asking the Lord's help to achieve these goals.

Another suggestion is to write your goals on a 3 x 5 card and put it in your wallet. Read it first thing in the morning, and then read it again every time you take a break. Do the same thing with your to-do list. Make it for each day. Review it in the morning and then review it throughout the day to keep yourself focused on the most important tasks you need to do.

Another important principle is always focusing on what you want, not on what you do not want. Your mind deliberates on where you focus your attention, and your unconscious does not understand negatives. Therefore, if your focus is on "I do not want to eat chocolate," the message received is "eat chocolate!" If I focus on "I cannot get further in debt," my thinking is focused on debt, not on wealth. Focus on your positive goals, focus on your priorities, focus on where you want to arrive, and that is where your mind will take you

2. Overcoming procrastination.

Procrastination is the enemy of action. One of the characteristics of successful people is that they act. They make decisions and act on those decisions, sometimes long before others have even thought about what to do. This is why they are often the ones to reap the benefits of their actions. One of the mottoes of the successful is "ready, *fire*, aim." That is, it is often more important to act than to be totally sure of your aim. This is not because they are unprepared, but rather, because they have prepared long and hard and therefore are ready when opportunity arises. Often when we see successful people we say, "Boy, was he lucky!" Was it luck or long preparation that allowed him to capture the moment? It is like seeing figure skating at the Olympics with the beautiful flowing movements, effortless jumps and twirls, and thinking it looks so easy. Then you get on the ice and you can barely stand up. It is the hundreds of hours of practice that allow the fluid, easy movements. This is true in any field. The more you practice, the easier it becomes. If you never start, you never will achieve your goal.

In *Secrets of the Millionaire Mind*, Harv Eker says, "The point is, however, that no luck—or anything else worthwhile—will come your way unless you take some form of action. To succeed financially, you have to do something, buy something or start something."[2]

When I think of a man of action, I think of the commander Moroni. He led his army to war, he found that the people did not support him, he did not pout or sit and complain, and he went back and motivated and galvanized the people with his standard of liberty. He acted without hesitation, without questioning himself, without discouragement. In his action he pulled the whole nation to success.

I, on the other hand, have not taken action so readily. I have begun diets "next Monday" at least a hundred times. By the time Monday comes around somehow I'm not quite ready, but who wants to start a diet on Tuesday? So it is next Monday again. Does this sound like a man of action? Who do you want to be?

> The road to success has many tempting parking spaces.
>
> —STEVE-POTTER

Many books on time management give suggestions on how to overcome procrastination. A first evaluation is to see if you procrastinate just some tasks or if you tend to put off most things. In the first case, the problem is probably technical—maybe you need to break down the task into smaller parts that are more manageable, or maybe there is some skill that you lack and you do not feel competent in that act. In the second case, the problems are psychological and you may want to review again if the goals you have set are really what you want. Julie Morgenstern in her book *Time Management from the Inside Out* gives eight suggestions for overcoming procrastination:

- Trust your instincts. You are probably over-rationalizing, or want to have all the information before making a decision. Remember ready, *fire,* aim. It is impossible to know everything; you must trust your instincts.
- Focus on your goal. Don't get bogged down in details or routine work, and don't deviate from where you want to go. If you refocus on your goals every day and you are committed to reaching those goals, you will be motivated to move ahead even when there are obstacles or you don't feel like doing the necessary steps.
- Break down overwhelming tasks into manageable parts. Don't

try to do everything at once, and don't be overwhelmed by the enormity of what you are trying to accomplish. Break down tasks into steps that you can obtain day by day.

- Combine a miserable task with something you enjoy. Every goal has actions that we may not enjoy, and we tend to put these off the most. In his book *Eat That Frog*, Brian Tracy states, "It has been said that if the first thing you do each morning is eat a live frog, you can go through the day with the satisfaction that that is probably the worst thing that is going to happen to you that day. Your 'frog' is your biggest, most important task, the one you are most likely to procrastinate on if you don't do something about it now. Discipline yourself to begin immediately and then to persist until the task is complete before you go on to something else. Here is a final observation: If you have to sit and eat a live frog, it doesn't pay to sit and look at it for very long!" Start with your least favorite but most important task and then reward yourself by following it with something you really like to do.
- Give yourself a time limit. If you break down the task into smaller units and give yourself a short time limit, you know that the torture will be over soon. Tell yourself that you will totally dedicate yourself to this project for thirty minutes and then you will do something you like. This focuses your attention and galvanizes your motivation, and the time will pass more quickly.
- Set your own deadline. Many people work better under pressure. Rather than work on deadlines imposed by others, establish your own deadlines and then see if you can beat them. If you have a project that you must finish by Friday, decide that you will do it by Wednesday evening and then throw yourself into it.
- Adopt a catch phrase. Give yourself a phrase, a ditty, or something to keep you focused. Phrases like "just do it," "let's get this done," or "let's get a move on" can keep us focused and motivated.[3]

If you put into practice the idea of getting up early, being the first to work, and planning your day, you will not want to waste all that energy by then fiddling away your time, diddling around on unimportant tasks, or procrastinating the things you need to do.

3. Taking responsibility

To act means not to react. It means taking responsibility for your life, and this is one of the reasons that so many people do not act. When I make a decision, I am responsible for the consequences of that decision. If I let other people around me make decisions for me, then I always have someone to blame, and I do not feel like a failure. Thoughts like "I'm just not lucky" or "I cannot do anything about it" are indications that we have not accepted responsibility for our life. Does this sound like a man of God? The Lord has said very clearly in D&C 58:27–28: "For behold it is not meet that I should command you in all things; for he that is compelled in all things, the same is a slothful and not a wise servant; wherefore he receiveth no reward. Verily I say, men should be anxiously engaged in a good cause and do many things of their own free will, and bring to pass much righteousness."

We are not to be commanded in all things. We are to act on our own. Agency is a gift that most people deny themselves. Every time I react to someone else's remarks, I have given him or her my agency. Every time I blame my boss, my wife, or traffic for my irritable mood, I have given away my agency. Every time I blame the government, my boss, or anyone else, I am not taking responsibility. Life will only change when you change. Positive things will come to you when you act in such a way to enhance your living. Acting requires becoming proactive. We must take responsibility for our actions. If we make a mistake, so what? We can learn something from it and change. If we never act, we have truly failed. If you enter the race of life, whether you finish first or last, you have won. You have learned valuable lessons; you have changed the course of your life; you have succeeded. The only loser is the person who never participated in the race.

We must learn that the only person we can control is ourselves, and the only way we can control a situation is through our own actions and behaviors. If your children cause you stress, you must change your actions as a parent. Trying to change your children is an act of coercion and is against the Lord's plan. We learn, however, that when we change, others change too. No one else causes your stress. No one else causes you to overeat. You are responsible for your actions and for your emotions. When we arrive at the judgment seat and ask the Lord why others had success and we did not, what do you think the Lord will say? Will he say, "I didn't want you to have success"? Or will he say, "They acted; you didn't. They put together a plan to better themselves and their situation and you sat there and complained. They followed the laws on which all blessings are predicated, and you didn't"?

All action must begin now. You have a plan that you have carefully worked out. You have the faith and desire. You must act now.

Talking doesn't cook rice.

—CHINESE PROVERB

---

4. Diligence

The Lord uses the word *diligence* repeatedly in the scriptures. You must earn your success. Nothing comes without hard work, and there is no work harder than changing yourself and your habits. No athlete expects success if he has not put in hundreds of hours of effort, sweat, and toil, yet somehow many people believe that success should come without effort. They expect their relationships to be perfect, their children to be disciplined, and their finances to bloom and grow without any effort. Study the lives of great men and women and you will see years of work, habits of self-discipline, and great diligence. Diligence is "steady, earnest and energetic application and effort." Look at your life. Look at the goals you are trying to achieve. Are you working toward those objectives steadily, day by day? Are you putting forth earnest and energetic application? Are you really making the effort? Nothing good comes easy. All jobs, no matter how much they correspond with your dreams, have aspects that just require hard work. There are jobs that may be boring, repetitive, or difficult that just require steadfastness and hard work. The Lord commanded Adam: "By the sweat of thy face shalt thou eat bread" (Moses 4:25). Diligence is sticking with your project no matter how difficult the road becomes.[4]

The quality of a person's life will be determined by the depth of their commitment to excellence, no matter what their chosen field.[5]

—VINCE LOMBARDI

Some people mistake diligence for the effort of doing something. "I tend the children every day. I am with them all day long." Part of diligence is doing things the right way. I can practice a free throw shot in basketball one hundred or five hundred times a day, but if I haven't put in the effort to correct my technique and practice the proper way of shooting, I am actually doing myself harm. If I do not practice good parenting skills, then I am reinforcing bad or mediocre skills that will not lead to a better relationship with my children. Often diligence must include an intelligent effort to find the right way to do things. Diligence means a commitment to excellence. We must not just act, but act to the best of our abilities. We must try for perfection in what we do. Do not commit to just being a better parent, but commit to being an excellent parent. On the job, commit to being among the top 10 percent in your field. Then go and learn how to do it and work until you achieve your goal. The Lord has not asked us to be mediocre people, but to be the best we can be.

> If a man is called to be a street sweeper he should sweep streets even as Michelangelo painted, or Beethoven composed music, or Shakespeare wrote poetry. He should sweep streets so well that all the hosts of heaven and earth will pause to say, "Here lived a great street sweeper who did his job well."[6]
>
> —MARTIN LUTHER KING JR.

ACTION EXERCISES

1. Examine your behaviors related to your goals. Which are the tasks that you tend to put off? What are you not doing that you should? What causes you the most difficulty? Write down your observations.
2. Make a commitment to yourself that you will succeed and you will overcome these difficulties.
3. Is your progress hindered because you need to learn new skills? Go back and make learning these skills part of your action plan, and start working today to improve them.
4. Decide that today, not tomorrow or next Monday or January 1, you will take one of these tasks and begin to work on it.
5. Review the section on procrastination and put into practice at least one suggestion.

6. Learn to eat your "frog" first thing in the morning.
7. Read books on time management and procrastination.
8. Examine whether you are a complainer or a doer. Accept responsibility for your actions. Make the important decisions of your life and begin today.
9. Be a doer. Take action. Begin now. Commit to excellence!
10. Select your favorite prophets or role models and read often what they did to take action and succeed.

Notes

1. Brian Tracy, *Million Dollar Habits* (Canada: Entrepreneur Press, 2004).
2. Harv Eker, *Secrets of the Millionaire Mind* (New York: Harper Business, 2005).
3. Julie Morgenstern, *Organizing from the Inside Out* (New York: Henry Holt & Co. LLC, 1998).
4. *Merriam-Webster Dictionary* (New York, Simon & Schuster, 1974).
5. Brian Tracy, *Change Your Thinking Change Your Life* (Hoboken, NJ: John Wiley & Sons, Inc., 2003).
6. Hal Urban, *Choices That Change Lives* (New York: Simon & Schuster, 2006), 145.

STEP 4

ENDURE TO THE END

This last step will take you to the top. As you are now putting into practice the habits of success and acting on your plan, you need to stop periodically and evaluate if you are still on course. Are you focused on your goals? Are your goals still the direction you wish to take? A further evaluation examines whether your actions and goals are in harmony with your values and beliefs.

You need to act with diligence. You need to endure to the end and persevere in the face of adversity. You need to grow step by step until you come to a fulness of success. Finally, you need to exercise patience to be flexible to change your course according to new needs and information.

Once you reach success, you need to learn the principle of gratitude and learn to reach for new summits. You will learn that success is a path to follow, not a place to arrive and sit down after your efforts.

THE STEPS TO SUCCESS

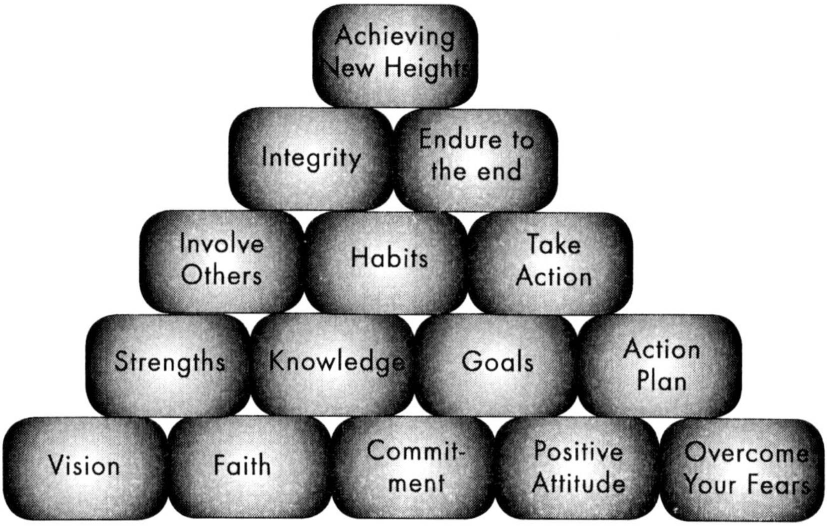

13 INTEGRITY

Hast thou considered my servant Job, that there is none like him in the earth, a perfect and upright man, one that feareth God, and escheweth evil? And still he holdeth fast his integrity, although thou movest me against him to destroy him without cause.

—JOB 2:3

As we actively work toward our goals and put into practice all the different steps of our action plan, we must stop occasionally and evaluate our progress. We may need to modify our goals, add new facets that were missing in our plan, or revise our timing. We may need to go back and reestablish our commitment and motivation to the goal and ask again for help from the Lord and our dream team. Part of this evaluation must be to verify if our actions are aligned with our basic principles. Are we holding true to a course that reflects who we are and what we deeply believe in? Are we acting with integrity?

This is one of the last bricks in your foundation for success—aligning your action with your values. This is called integrity. Integrity is completely following the principles we believe in, whether or not other people are watching. If you believe in honesty, you must be honest in all circumstances without compromise. Great leaders and successful people have integrity.

Can you think of any prophet who did not show integrity? Someone who was wishy-washy in his fundamental principles? Can you think of any great leader who did not stand for integrity? The most beloved presidents of the United States are Abraham Lincoln and George Washington. Lincoln was known as Honest Abe, and Washington is famous for chopping down the cherry tree and not being able to tell a lie. Think of Ghandi, Martin Luther King Jr., or Nelson Mandela. Think of the

Prophet Joseph Smith. These are men who put their integrity to the test with years of prison or their own life.

Nothing is at last sacred but the integrity of your own mind.[1]

—RALPH WALDO EMERSON

Many people believe that if you want worldly success you need to follow the ways of the world through deceit, dishonesty, and taking advantage of others. This is their excuse either to not search for success, or to justify their dishonest behavior. Nothing can be further from the truth. The quality that is most valued in most companies is integrity. All business is founded on some form of relationship—the relationship of the company to costumers, to society, or to the government. Equally important is the relationship between the leaders of the company and the employees, between supervisor and employee, between coworkers, between the employee and the company. These relationships are the foundation of business, and all relationships are built on trust. Trust is formed through honesty and integrity. Many studies have shown that the companies with the highest level of trust among their customers are the companies that have success. This trust is called reputation, and it is extremely valuable whether you are a company, government, parent, spouse, church member, or individual.

Fame is a vapor, popularity an accident, riches take wings, those who cheer today will curse tomorrow; only one thing endures—character.[2]

—HORACE GREELY

Do you do an honest day's work for your pay? One study shows that the average worker only actively works 50 percent of the time.[1] Thirty-seven percent of the time is wasted in idle conversation with coworkers, and 13 percent is wasted by arriving late, leaving early, extending lunch and coffee breaks, and so on. Even most managers admitted that they only spent half of their time working on company business. If 50 percent is the average, it means that many people are not even working 50 percent of the time. Is this honesty? It also means that if you apply the virtue of honesty and put in 100 percent of your time on the job, you will accomplish twice as much as the other workers and will eventually be recognized for your work habits and be promoted.[3]

If integrity is living up to the values you prize the most, you have to be aware of what your top values really are. It is surprising that many people aren't sure just what their top values really are. We profess values that are not necessarily what we really care about the most. Try doing this exercise. Try writing down *your* seven most important values and ideals and then put them in order or priority. You may use the below list of different personality characteristics and values to decide what is most important to you. If you have difficulty seeing these values for yourself, ask yourself what do you most admire in other people. Pick the seven that you value the most.

Value list

Empathy, honesty, love, mutual communication, sincerity, desire for knowledge, righteousness, respect, fun-loving, achievement, peaceful, nurturing, sense of humor, confidence, faith, trustworthiness, responsibility, charity, goodness, family oriented, adventurous, hospitable, courageous, humility, greed, resourcefulness, enthusiasm, initiative, cleverness, style, rationality, emotionality, logic, intelligence, peaceful, friendliness, morality, passion, creativity, supportiveness, compassion, meekness, spirituality, energy, inspiration, charm, social graces, altruism, arrogance, zeal, decisiveness, self-sufficiency, neediness, integrity, cheerfulness, being laid-back, driven, tidiness, neat, purity, attractiveness, capable, proud, understanding, career-oriented, dedication, inventive, thoughtfulness, studious, warmness, people-orientation, task-orientation, education, faithfulness, loyalty, love of nature, spontaneous, teamwork, love of animals, search for excellence, fame, glory, money, social acknowledgement, cleanliness, moderation, balance, grace, knowledge, athletic, poised . . .

You complete the list.

To put these in order, first write on a sheet of paper the seven you think are the most important, whether from this list or your own ideas. Then select any two and compare them. Is love more important than respect? If it is, then you can compare this to the next on your list and so on until you have created a hierarchy from what is most important to you to what is least. Now write them down.

My ideals and values:

1.
2.
3.
4.
5.
6.
7.

Now the question is, are you living these values? If you have family as one of your top values, how much time and energy do you really dedicate to your family? If you believe in honesty, are you always honest and sincere?

If integrity is important in business, just think how important it is in our intimate relationships. All love between a husband and wife is based on trust. Betrayal of trust ruins the relationship—it's that simple. One of the first principles in parenting is that if you make a promise you must keep it, and the corollary is, do not make promises you may not be able to keep. This is a question of integrity. It is easy to lie to our children to keep them quiet or happy, but over time they lose that trust in what you say, and it is very difficult to rebuild it. Integrity is also living the values you teach to your children. They know when you're not living your values. Not living the values you teach is called hypocrisy, and it seems that teenagers have special antennae for beaming in on parental hypocrisy.

One of the reasons we become discouraged with ourselves is that we do not live up to what we believe in. When you have started a diet thirty times and have always failed in the first few days, you lose confidence in yourself because you realize that you are not living up to your potential. You do not have integrity. You lie to yourself.

We are not necessarily born with all virtues. Learning to be virtuous is a choice. Hyrum Smith Jr. tells of Ben Franklin, who chose twelve virtues to develop in his life: temperance, silence, order, resolution, frugality, industry, sincerity, justice, moderation, cleanliness, tranquility, and chastity. Franklin defined each virtue with a written statement. For example, for temperance he wrote, "Eat not to dullness; drink not to elevation." For sincerity he wrote, "Use no hurtful deceit; think innocently and justly, and if you speak, speak accordingly." He showed his list to a Quaker friend who added the quality of humility, stating that Franklin showed little and needed to improve that virtue. Franklin then divided each year into thirteen weekly cycles and dedicated each week to intensely focusing on one of these virtues. He repeated this each year for all the years of his life. At the age of seventy-eight he wrote: "On the whole, tho' I never arrived at the Perfection I had been so ambitious of obtaining, but fell far short of it, yet I was by the Endeavor a better and happier Man than I otherwise should have been, if I had not attempted it." The only virtue that he didn't feel he had much success with was humility.[4]

We would do well to follow Benjamin Franklin's example. Pick the virtues that you feel you should most develop; ask your spouse or a good friend what you should add to the list, and then systematically make an effort to put these into practice. Dedicate a week or a month at a time for the rest of your life to focus on each virtue and put it into practice. Like Franklin, we may not arrive at perfection, but we will be "a better and happier" person for having tried.

Only the good can be happy, and only the virtuous can be good.[5]

—ARISTOTLE

If we want to be happy, we must develop a virtuous life. Search for the values and virtues that you admire the most in others and ask yourself if you are living those same virtues. If not, start today.

The key to developing these virtues in our life is self-discipline. Self-discipline goes hand in hand with integrity. Aristotle taught again that if you do not have a particular virtue, you can obtain it by practicing. If you act as if you had that virtue you will obtain it.

Elbert Hubbard, a twentieth century writer, said, "Self-discipline is the ability to make yourself do what you should do, when you should do it, whether you want to or not."[6] David O. McKay stated that "self-discipline is spirituality," no more, no less.[7]

Taking Aristotle's belief to heart, if you want to develop courage, begin to consciously act courageously each time you find yourself in a fearful situation. As you control and determine these behaviors, you are in fact developing courage. Repeat it for the next virtue you have decided to develop. Determine what behaviors make up that virtue and start imitating those behaviors. Act as if you are already that way and that is what you will become. If you wish to develop meekness, a virtue that is repeatedly mentioned in the scriptures, determine what behaviors make up meekness and begin putting them into practice.

Do not be discouraged in your quest for virtue and integrity. Just as Benjamin Franklin made developing twelve virtues a lifelong quest, most of us will need to make achieving success a lifetime quest. But it is the quest that will make all the difference in whatever endeavor we pursue, whether spiritual or material.

ACTION EXERCISES

1. Determine your top values. Write in your diary how well you are living those values. Evaluate any discrepancies between what you have identified as a top value and the time you dedicate to it or how you live it.
2. Determine the values and virtues you would like to improve in your life and write them down. Write a short description near each one to describe it.
3. Identify the behaviors that compose that virtue, and which behaviors you need to improve.
4. Find quotes, books, role models, and scriptures that relate to each of those virtues.
5. Dedicate one week at a time to study each virtue. Meditate on it and practice the behaviors of that virtue. Act as if you are already that way.
6. Every evening in your prayers, evaluate if you have lived according to your values and if you are living the virtues that you most want to acquire.

Note

1. Available from www.brainyquote.com.
2. Brian Tracy, *Million Dollar Habits* (Canada: Entrepreneur Press, 2004).
3. Ibid.
4. Hyrum Smith, *The Ten Natural Laws of Successful Time and Life Management* (New York: Warner Books, 1994).
5. Available from www.brainyquote.com.
6. Available from www.ordinarypoeplecanwin.com.
7. Clare Middlemiss, *Teachings of President David O. McKay* (Salt Lake City: Deseret Book, 1967).

14 ENDURE TO THE END

He that is faithful and endureth shall overcome the world.
—D&C 63:47

Anyone who has tried to reach a goal knows that things do not go according to plan. We decide to exercise regularly, and after a few runs we get tendonitis, or we decide to hold family prayer every evening and our son now has basketball practice and returns late. Often, it seems that as soon as you schedule something, all forces start to work against you. You are right—they do. God wants you to succeed, but Satan certainly does not, and it is not by chance that one of his names is the adversary. When all goes wrong, you can be assured that you have chosen to do the right thing.

There is no education like adversity.[1]
—BENJAMIN DISRAELI

We are on this earth to test our faith, and much of the test is to see if we will continue working toward our goals when things go wrong. In the words of Winston Churchill: "Never, never, never, never give up."

Several studies have been done regarding success and, in particular, financial success. In the book *The Millionaire Mind*, the author analyzed all the factors that make up the success of the typical millionaire in America.[2] He found that intelligence is not a factor. Some successful people are very intelligent, but the vast majority are not. Even creativity is not an important aspect for most. The two characteristics that stand out if someone wants success are diligence and persistence. Most millionaires are owners of small companies, stores, or commercial activities, usually in rural areas, that for years have worked hard and diligently, who have been frugal with their money, reinvesting it in their activity, and who have been persistent. It was found that most of them have gone through difficult times, but they persisted anyway. They were constant in their commitment. They overcame all adversity by constant and persistent work. Most did not arrive at that mythical million dollars until the end of their careers that spanned many decades. Unlike them, many of us give up the struggle, sometimes right before we would have had success.

In *10 Steps to Better Parenting,* the authors interviewed hundreds of youth and parents of the Church in three different countries. In particular they talked with young men and women in their twenties who had left home, and asked what were the best memories they had and what they wished their parents would have done differently. Surprisingly, a good number talked about how family home evenings with their families are among their best memories, even though they didn't like it at the time and complained about it. Many others stated that they wished that their parents had continued holding it in their home.[3]

Often we do not see the results of what we are doing while we do it. It seems that every family home evening is a struggle and none of the children care; all they do is fight. Instead, if we persevere with faith in what the Lord has promised, even in the face of apparent indifference, we will succeed.

Last summer, Fernanda and I were hiking up a mountain that was much more difficult to climb than we expected. Each turn of the trail revealed the path that just kept going up and up, and we were tired. We kept hoping that the trail would level off; instead it just got steeper and steeper. Finally we called it quits and went back down the mountain. From the bottom looking up, we realized that we had quit right below the peak of the mountain. If we had continued another fifteen or twenty minutes, we would have reached the top and had a magnificent view. It made me think how often we come close to a goal but give up because the road seems too difficult. Often we may be very close to reaching the peak, but we do not persevere and we miss many opportunities.

The Lord uses the term "enduring to the end" eleven times just in the Doctrine and Covenants. He never says "endure *almost* to the end," or "endure while the going is easy." We must hang in there, overcome all obstacles, and persevere through defeat and difficulties. Only then will we have our prize.

> And again I would that ye should learn that he only is saved that endureth unto the end. Even so. Amen.
>
> —D&C 53:7

You will fail often. But success is getting up one more time and continuing your struggle. Each time you act, you are creating new neural pathways. It is not true that having acted was a waste of time, because subtle changes are occurring in your brain. When you are trying to break a bad habit, like swearing, you will fail repeatedly. But it is not an all-or-nothing deal. Each failure gives you the opportunity to revise your plan and see what went wrong. You might find that swearing is not the major problem—it's the anger that precedes it. But every time you succeed, every time you stop yourself, you change your neurological wiring. Alternative pathways are established. The more you practice those pathways, the stronger they will get. You cannot expect to succeed right away, but each small success builds on the last one until those alternative pathways become predominate.

> The test of success is not what you do when you are on top. Success is how high you bounce when you hit bottom.[4]
>
> —GENERAL GEORGE S. PATTON

The same is true with dieting, getting up early, or any form of self-discipline. It is a process. Acting, failing, getting up, and acting again until you start changing your momentum is the key to any enterprise. There are two laws of physic at work here. The first is the law of inertia. When a body is at rest, it will tend to stay at rest. The second is the law of momentum—bodies in motion will stay in motion. It is extremely difficult to overcome inertia. When NASA sent its first manned spacecraft to the moon, 95 percent of the energy necessary for the entire trip of 340,000 miles was used to lift off and send the spacecraft up the first 100 miles.[5] The same is true with any new habit you begin or any new activity or enterprise. It is the first month or two that will consume 95 percent of your energy. You are working against inertia. You are trying to move an enormous weight. Once you get it rolling, however, the law of momentum takes over and what seemed insurmountable in the beginning gets easier as time goes on. You have built new muscles, new neural pathways, and new habits of success.

What has to carry you through during this process is the desire you started with, the dream you have, and the commitment you made to yourself, to the Lord, and to others. This is the moment when you need the help of others. If you are a frustrated parent and you have tried good strategies but nothing seems to be working, and the children's behavior gets worse rather than better (and it will in the beginning!), you need to enlist the help of others. Go to the Lord with your concerns; seek his help and support. Almost always, however, the Lord works through other people. You need their help. You need your spouse or a parent to support you. If they aren't available, you need a friend or neighbor. You need help and this should be part of your action plan.

The same is true of any endeavor. Seek the help of the Lord, but seek help close at hand to help you through the difficulties. Find someone to exercise with, find someone to talk to, find a mentor, or find someone who has been through the same experience. In all groups for recovering addiction, the most important aspect of the group is the buddy system, having someone you can go to when you just cannot handle the situation anymore.

The saying that behind every great man there is a great woman is true, but it's not just true for men. There is always someone behind the person of success who gave the moral support, the emotional uplift to see the person of success (whether man or woman) through the difficult times.

When we work toward success, we must have patience and trust in the Lord. Look at Job. For no apparent reason he lost his riches, his house, his children. His wife turned against him as did his friends, and he was afflicted with boils. He endured all this and persevered with faith in the Lord.

Every failure teaches a man something if he will learn.[6]

—CHARLES DICKENS

Often, however, when the going gets tough and things are not working out, it is not because the Lord is testing us but because we have left out one or more fundamental steps in our preparation. Obstacles give us the chance to reevaluate our action plan. Do we have adequate preparation for what we are doing? Have we read enough books? Have we sought out the counsel of experts in the field? The number one reason most businesses fail is that the owners did not have adequate knowledge to deal with important aspects of that business. Maybe you need to team up with someone who has abilities that you lack. Maybe you didn't have the proper funds to see you through the difficult times.

Rick Pittino, the well-known basketball coach, in his book *Success Is a Choice* explains that when a game is difficult and the other team has the advantage, this is the time to go back to the game plan and restart with the fundamentals.[7] You go to the plays that you have practiced hundreds of times. You go to your strengths. The same is true in life, and this is why success has to start from the inside out. Often you have to go back to your dream, where you started, to the commitment you made and make sure that you still have that burning desire. You have to evaluate if you have developed the proper virtues and skills necessary for this endeavor. Very often the Lord sends us difficulties for this very reason—we need to develop other strengths before we can succeed in what we desire. We have to go back to our strengths. We will succeed only if we are using those talents and abilities that make us unique. We have to evaluate our plan of action and our timetable.

All difficulties are opportunities for growth and for learning. Therefore, perhaps the most important foundation we have to review is our attitudes and beliefs. If we are positive, we will find opportunity in the midst of defeat. Remember that on the average all millionaires have gone bankrupt at least twice in their career. The difference between them and everyone else is that they get back up, learn from their mistakes, and use this new knowledge to succeed. They have faith that they will succeed, they have a winning mentality, and they persevere.

Paul Harvey, news analyst and author, said, "Someday I hope to enjoy enough of what the world calls success so that someone will ask me, 'What's the secret of it?' I shall say simply this: 'I get up when I fall down.' "[8]

None of the prophets had it easy. Nephi was threatened repeatedly by his brothers and almost killed several times. He had to build the ship to carry his family to the promised land. He had to create a town and survive in the wilderness. He had to defend his people against his brothers, and he had to keep them righteous through his own example and his teachings. Joseph Smith's struggles were similar to Nephi's. He took his people into the wilderness and fought against persecution. Or, we can take the example of Paul, who was thrown into prison repeatedly, was threatened with his life, and traveled thousands of miles to preach the gospel to different peoples and cultures. But he was able to say, "I have fought a good fight" (Hebrews 4:7).

The Lord has said that we must persevere to the end. Most of us had faith sufficient to be baptized. For the rest of our lives we must keep the faith through all the difficulties that life presents, and endure to the end.

> The beauty of the soul shines out when a man bears with composure one heavy mischance after another, not because he does not feel them, but because he is man of high and heroic temper.[9]
>
> —ARISTOTLE

Fundamental to any plan for success is finding a way to overcome discouragement. There will be times when everything is working against you and you feel depressed and discouraged. What do you do?

Any recovering addict knows that even if they no longer drink or use drugs or gamble, the battle is not over. They know that they have to live their life one day at a time and always be conscious of their addiction. They know that all it takes is one moment of weakness and despair and they can start all over again and send their lives reeling out of control. Is it so different for any of us? Maybe it is even more difficult for us because we do not have that awareness of how the little things in our lives can defeat our plans and ruin our goals.

The work of life and the road to success require that we gradually take control of all areas of our life. All the projects that I want to accomplish tomorrow will be compromised if I make the bad decision to stay up late and watch a rerun or a stupid film today. It might not seem that important at the time, but tomorrow I just won't have the energy to accomplish what I want to do. I will be tired and irritable and won't have the patience to cope with my children, and I will lose it and fall back into my old patterns of screaming at them. In a way, we are all recovering addicts, trying to overcome our old patterns of behavior and of thought. We must fight the battle daily to achieve the success of overcoming our natural tendencies and allowing our spirit to command our actions.

When we realize that every day we need to keep marching up the hill of success and the mountain of our personal progress or else we will lose our balance and fall down a few steps, we will seek all the help we can get. We will constantly search for better ways to achieve our goals, we will read the scriptures to have inspiration and motivation, we will focus on improving our health to have more energy, and we will constantly pray for the Lords' support. Enduring to the end does not mean reaching a ledge and just staying there. We cannot remain stationary in life or in our eternal progress. Enduring to the end means steadily, step-by-step, moving up the mountain. Maybe some days you will leap up several steps with enthusiasm and other days you will move barely an inch. Sometimes you will slip and fall, but you get up and carry on. It means finding a way around all the obstacles so that you can continue your journey even if it means taking a detour and retracing your steps to find a better. It means never, never giving up.

ACTION EXERCISES

1. Examine all the obstacles that you can foresee in achieving your goal, and determine how you are going to overcome each obstacle. Write down your plan in your personal diary.
2. Determine what you are going to do when you become discouraged. How are you going to lift your spirits?
3. Identify whom you can go to when you are in the midst of a crisis. Who will be your buddy? Go to them beforehand and let them know why you need them and explain how they can help.
4. Read the scriptures and pray to the Lord for help every day.
5. Pick some special scriptures, quotes, and stories that are inspirational to you and put them where you can see them.

Notes

1. Available from www.brainyquote.com.
2. Thomas J. Stanley, *The Millionaire Mind* (Kansas City, MO: Andrews McMeel Publishing, 2000).

3. Brent L. Top and Bruce A. Chadwick, *10 Secrets Wise Parents Know* (Salt Lake City: Deseret Book, 2004).
4. Art Mortell, *The Courage to Fail* (New York: McGraw-Hill, Inc., 1993).
5. Brian Tracy, *Million Dollar Habits* (Canada: Entrepreneur Press, 2004).
6. Available from www.brainyquote.com.
7. Rick Pittino, *Success Is a Choice* (New York: Broadway Books, 1997).
8. Brian Tracy, Ibid.
9. Available from www.brainyquote.com.

15 ACHIEVING NEW HEIGHTS

He that is faithful and endureth shall overcome the world.

—D&C 63:47

You have now arrived. You have overcome your fears; you have faced adversity and succeeded. You have reached your goal. You have climbed the mountain of success and you have reached the peak. Now what? Are you ready for your crown of righteousness?

Rick Pittino again states that "the greatest hurdle you must face is surviving success itself."[1] Why should success be a problem? Isn't that what we have been working toward all this time? Yet, we can look to many entertainers, sports figures, businesses, and others and see that as soon as they achieve success they start sliding, they no longer produce the same quality product, and they forget what brought them to their achievement. So, although you have been working hard to achieve your goals and should feel a sense of accomplishment when you arrive, there are many pitfalls inherent in achieving success. We will examine three and see what we can do to overcome them.

The first pitfall is pride. Too often when we achieve success of any kind we attribute our success to our superior abilities, diligence, and hard work. The Book of Mormon is replete with examples of the Nephites prospering in the land and then being lifted up in pride and turning away from God. One of the most obvious examples is that of the Zoramites and the tower of Rameumpton in the city of Antionum. Alma and two of his sons went to preach to the Zoramites and found that within their synagogue they had erected a tower called Rameumpton from which they would take turns, one at a time, praying with their arms outstretched toward heaven saying,

"Holy God, we believe that thou hast separated us from our brethren. But we believe that thou has elected us to be thy holy children. And again we thank thee, O God, that we are a chosen and a holy people. Amen" (Alma 31:16, 18). Alma was astonished and called them a wicked people. We may be astonished too, but don't most people do much the same?

Isn't it human nature to take for granted that the material things we have gained are due to our labors alone, and to our superior abilities, and we therefore deserve everything we have obtained? The equally logical conclusion is that those people who have not achieved what we have are just not as diligent, intelligent, or as capable as we are. The poor deserve to be poor because they are lazy. The overweight and fat people just don't have our self-control, and the parents of delinquent children didn't know how to parent. There are several hundred references to pride in the scriptures; the following is just one:

> And it came to pass in the eighth year of the reign of the judges, that the people of the church began to wax proud, because of their exceeding riches, and their fine silks, and their fine-twined linen, and because of their many flocks and herds, and their gold and their silver, and all manner of precious things, which they had obtained by their industry; and in all these things were they lifted up in the pride of their eyes, for they began to wear very costly apparel. (Alma 4:6)

Pride is not just about worldly goods. We can be overcome by pride in many different ways. Pride is taking credit for deeds that only in part are the results of our efforts. We when we are prideful, we ignore the blessings of the Lord, the help of friends, and the sustaining effort of our family. Pride means feeling superior to others for what we have achieved. As C. S. Lewis states, "Pride gets no pleasure out of having something, only out of having more of it than the next man. We say that people are proud of being rich, or clever, or good-looking, but they are not. They are proud of being richer, cleverer, or better-looking than others. If every one else became equally rich, or clever, or good-looking there would be nothing to be proud about. It is the comparison that makes you proud: the pleasure of being above the rest. Once the element of competition has gone, pride has gone."[2]

There has been no better talk about pride than that of President Ezra Taft Benson in the April conference in 1989:

> When pride has a hold on our hearts, we lose our independence of the world and deliver our freedoms to the bondage of men's judgment. The world shouts louder than the whisperings of the Holy Ghost. The reasoning of men overrides the revelations of God, and the proud let go

> of the iron rod. (See 1 Ne. 8:19–28; 1 Ne. 11:25; 1 Ne. 15:23–24.)
>
> Pride is a sin that can readily be seen in others but is rarely admitted in ourselves. Most of us consider pride to be a sin of those on the top, such as the rich and the learned, looking down at the rest of us. (See 2 Ne. 9:42.) There is, however, a far more common ailment among us—and that is pride from the bottom looking up. It is manifest in so many ways, such as faultfinding, gossiping, backbiting, murmuring, living beyond our means, envying, coveting, withholding gratitude and praise that might lift another, and being unforgiving and jealous. . . . The proud depend upon the world to tell them whether they have value or not. Their self-esteem is determined by where they are judged to be on the ladders of worldly success. They feel worthwhile as individuals if the numbers beneath them in achievement, talent, beauty, or intellect are large enough. Pride is ugly. It says, "If you succeed, I am a failure."[3]

A good example of this from the scriptures is Jonah. He went to preach to the wicked city of Nineveh, prophesying all the calamities that would occur if the people did not repent. Then they did repent; he was successful. Did he rejoice? No. The scriptures say, "But it displeased Jonah exceedingly, and he was very angry" (Jonah 4:1). He found no joy in their repentance, but rather wanted to feel superior to them.

How do we avoid the pitfall of pride in our life? One way is recognizing the hand of the Lord in all things. We must have the humility to know that we are only partly responsible for our success. We must recognize the help of the Lord and those who have helped us, and be grateful. Sincere gratitude is the mark of humility. One way to develop this is to thank people for what they do. Create a habit of thankfulness. Husbands, thank your wife when she cooks you breakfast; thank her for the work she does. Wives, thank your husband for his support and work. Thank your children for the joy they bring to your life. Thank your supervisor and coworkers when they help you; thank your employees for the work they do. Learn to recognize and be thankful for all those positive things that occur in your life. Another way to develop this is to keep a gratitude diary. Write down every day, or frequently, all the blessings you have received, all the good things that have occurred, and express your gratitude. This helps you both to focus on the positive in your life and to develop a grateful spirit. It also serves when you are feeling down to see all the blessings you have received. Enjoy your success, but be grateful. Be humble.

Another pitfall is that many reach the peak of the mountain and stop climbing. As soon as they stop climbing, they start sliding down. They no longer challenge themselves. They no longer put into practice the successful habits they had developed. They coast. How often have you gone on a diet, lost the weight you wanted, and then stopped putting into practice those good eating and exercise habits you had developed? What happens? Inevitably you put the weight right back on, and usually you will even add some more. The good thoughts and actions you have created must remain part of your life or you will slide right back down and often find your self worse off. Once you learn to better your parenting skills, you can't relax your guard and slip back into old habits because there will always be new challenges. Can you imagine someone on the job who obtains a promotion by successfully creating habits of hard work, coming in early, and developing good people skills, and then suddenly becomes slothful and lazy? Will that promotion last very long? The moral of the story is you can't stop. You can't stop your progress and your upward march or you will start sliding.

> March on. Do not tarry. To go forward is to move toward perfection. March on and fear not the thorns, or the sharp stones on life's path.[4]
>
> —KAHLIL GIBRAN

Some people's achievements exceed their expectations, so they make no further goals. It is important that when we reach a goal, when we feel successful, we examine what got us there. We must take inventory of what we did that was good and right, and continue doing those things. Decide what talents you have developed and what good habits you have created, and start examining how you can use these to achieve further goals. Examine how your goals have made you a better person and resolve to continue to keep those habits and expand them to continue your personal progress. Remember, we are working for eternal progress, not just one goal. Unfortunately we have examples of this too from the history of the Church. Think of Oliver Cowdery. Think of the revelations he received, the visitations from John the Baptist; Peter, James, and John; Elias; Moses; and even the Lord himself. What did he do? He thought he had reached the top. He thought he didn't need to climb further. He thought he was superior and had reached the summit. How far was his fall?

Finally reaching a goal, no matter how pleasant and sought after, almost always leads to an emotional letdown. The longer and harder you have worked for that accomplishment, the more emotionally drained you will be. I have worked with adult education with the military and their family members most of my life, and many of my students have been taking classes for eight, ten, or fifteen years to receive their bachelor's degree. They have had to take a course here and there between one military mission and another. They have taken courses in remote locations or in war zones like Bosnia, Iraq, or Afghanistan. They have taken many courses online through distant education and others in small classrooms without any of the usual visual aids college students are use to. Most of my students are soldiers who get up at 5 AM to report to PT at six, go through their work day until 5 PM, and then take three-hour evening courses until 9:30 before they go home to their families. Somewhere they have to fit in homework. They face their fears and persevere, and finally reach the goal that they committed to so many years before. They have been looking forward to this moment for much of their career, and even though they are content to have reached it, there is a sense of letdown. Why?

As humans, we tend to think that it is the goal that will bring us happiness. We think in terms like, "When I am skinny, *then* I will be happy. When I have that new car, new house, a million dollars, *then* I will be happy. When my children do not fight all the time, *then* I will feel blessed. Just as soon as I get promoted, or get my degree, *then* I will be satisfied with myself."

The problem, of course, is that none of these things by themselves bring happiness. When we reach our goal we realize that we still aren't any happier, or maybe we should say that once the momentary joy of reaching our goal is over, we have that pervading sense of disappointment. This is one reason people do not succeed in the first place. They are afraid of reaching their goal because then they have to face the reality that it was not the extra weight, lack of money, or screaming children that made them unhappy.

How often have we seen athletes, entertainers, or movie stars reach success and then throw it away by excess drinking, drugs, or just poor performance? Worldly success by itself does not bring happiness. If you were not happy before, you will not be happy after reaching your goal.

There is only one way to prevent this: to see your life as a journey—a never-ending process of reaching for the stars, climbing the mountain, and then finding that there are other mountains to climb. The peak we see in front of us is really just a small plateau that leads upward to other peaks and higher summits to conquer.

This is true success: undertaking the journey of self-discovery, self-mastery, and self-improvement that lasts a lifetime and beyond. As we achieve each goal, our faith in the Lord expands and our self-esteem is enhanced. When we recognize in our lives the support, the trust, and the active help of the people close to us, we become ever more grateful and our ability to love increases. The more successful we are, the more we have a duty to reach down and help others to arrive at the same peaks and experience the same joy, and even stimulate them to go higher than we can. There is no envy, there is no competition, but there is only the desire to have others experience our joy. This is God's formula for success.

ACTION EXERCISES

1. Plan what you want to do to celebrate your success.
2. Make an inventory of the skills you have acquired to obtain this success.
3. Make an inventory of the people that have helped you. Express to them your sincere gratitude.
4. Guard against pride.
5. Begin a gratitude journal in which you write down all the blessings and good things that you experience.
6. Express your thankfulness to the Lord daily in your prayers.
7. Begin a new list of goals and new action plans to reach new peaks of success.
8. Look how you can help others in reaching their goals.

The only true measure of success is the ratio between what we might have done and what we might have been on one hand, and the things that we have done and the things we have made of ourselves on the other.[5]

—H. G. WELLS

Note

1. Rick Pittino, *Success Is a Choice* (New York: Broadway Books, 1997).
2. C.S. Lewis, *Mere Christianity* (New York: The Macmillian Co., 1949).
3. Ezra Taft Benson, "Beware of Pride," *Ensign*, May 1989, 4.
4. Brian Tracy, *Million Dollar Habits* (Canada: Entrepreneur Press, 2004).
5. Brian Tracy, *Change Your Thinking Change Your Life* (Hoboken, New Jersey: John Wiley & Sons, Inc., 2003), 222.

INDEX

L

M

N

O

P

R

S

Trafford R. Cole is a clinical psychologist. He graduated from Padua University in Italy in 1982 and did post-graduate training in marriage counseling and sex therapy. After several years of private practice, he began teaching psychology courses for the European division of the University of Maryland. He has taught U.S. military members and dependents at several bases in northern Italy for the last twenty years. He enriched his experience by working for several years for the Army Family Advocacy Program as an educator, teaching courses on parenting, relationship enrichment, stress management, and child abuse recognition.

He has also worked as a professional genealogist for Italy and has written numerous articles on the topic. His book *Italian Genealogical Records* has remained a classic in the field of Italian genealogy.

He presently lives in Italy with his wife, Fernanda, and his three sons, Joel, Jeffrey, and Jason.

0 26575 70916 2